"There are times when actions matter most. There are even times when your mere presence matters most. But as Marshall and Newheiser make clear, our lives are filled with times 'when words matter most.' This book is for those times. Written by women and for women, these pages are so saturated with Scripture and biblical wisdom that they can be equally beneficial to men. *When Words Matter Most* can serve either for small-group study or personal reading. Most of us speak to one or more who are weary, wayward, or worried almost every day. Learning from the lessons and examples of this book will prepare you to be more effective when you do."

Don Whitney, Professor of Biblical Spirituality and Associate Dean, The Southern Baptist Theological Seminary; author, *Family Worship*; *Praying the Bible*; and *Spiritual Disciplines for the Christian Life*

"*When Words Matter Most* is a thoroughly practical and biblical book to help you speak the truth in love to others caught up in a variety of struggles. This book is engaging and very helpful. I highly recommend it."

Martha Peace, biblical counselor; author, *The Excellent Wife*

"We need each other to grow in Christ. We also need to hear God's word, and God uses others to speak that word to us. Marshall and Newheiser remind us of this fundamental but often ignored truth in this wonderfully practical book. We are all needy and weak. We all need to be encouraged and challenged, and we need to hear God's word practically applied to our lives by those who know us. We are confident that the Lord will use this book to help us walk worthily of the Lord who has called us to be like him."

Tom and Diane Schreiner, James Buchanan Harrison Professor of New Testament Interpretation, The Southern Baptist Theological Seminary; and his wife, Diane

"The riches of God's word should not be hoarded as a private treasure. This practical, powerful book challenges believers to allow Scripture's healing balm to flow naturally into our relationships and conversations. God's words matter more and accomplish more than our own. When the teaching of the Bible permeates our own thoughts, we can gently and powerfully share strengthening truth with one another."

Deborah Young, Chief Curriculum Officer, Bible Study Fellowship

"From the very beginning, God created mankind with the ability to communicate so man could commune with God and fellow man. However, because of sin, communication has been horribly corrupted. Cheryl Marshall and Caroline Newheiser have written a much-needed book to help restore gracious and loving communication to bring strength, comfort, and sometimes reproof to those who need it. Gracious speech full of truth is a lost art to this generation. *When Words Matter Most* is a carefully written resource to restore this vital and necessary practice."

John D. Street, Professor, The Master's University and Seminary; President, Association of Certified Biblical Counselors

"What a challenge it is to speak the truth in love to those whom the Lord places in our lives. It is much easier to just talk about comfortable topics and avoid the tough ones altogether. *When Words Matter Most* serves as a welcome tool to show us how to do the right thing and choose the words that matter most with utmost prayer and care. Marshall and Newheiser skillfully provide biblically saturated advice coupled with real-life examples from their vast experience. They do not seek to provide a formula for success, but rather carefully suggest methods to encourage the fainthearted and do so with grace. It is exciting to think about how the Lord may choose to use conversations we may be privileged to initiate to transform hearts and bring glory to his name. May we be eager for the task! This helpful book will spur us on in ways yet unseen with its well-organized categories of concern and corresponding biblical truth. I am grateful to both Marshall and Newheiser for this labor of love and gladly recommend it."

Mary Mohler, Director, Seminary Wives Institute, The Southern Baptist Theological Seminary; author, *Growing in Gratitude*

When Words Matter Most

When Words
Matter Most

Speaking Truth with Grace to Those You Love

Cheryl Marshall and
Caroline Newheiser

WHEATON, ILLINOIS

When Words Matter Most: Speaking Truth with Grace to Those You Love
Copyright © 2021 by Cheryl Marshall and Caroline Newheiser
Published by Crossway
   1300 Crescent Street
   Wheaton, Illinois 60187

Cover design: Crystal Courtney

First printing 2021

Printed in the United States of America

Unless otherwise indicated, Scripture quotations are from the ESV® Bible (The Holy Bible, English Standard Version®), copyright © 2001 by Crossway, a publishing ministry of Good News Publishers. Used by permission. All rights reserved.

Scripture quotations marked NASB are from *The New American Standard Bible*®. Copyright © 1960, 1962, 1963, 1968, 1971, 1972, 1973, 1975, 1977, 1995 by The Lockman Foundation. Used by permission. www.Lockman.org.

Scripture quotations marked (NIV) are taken from the Holy Bible, New International Version®, NIV®. Copyright © 1973, 1978, 1984, 2011 by Biblica, Inc.™ Used by permission of Zondervan. All rights reserved worldwide. www.zondervan.com. The "NIV" and "New International Version" are trademarks registered in the United States Patent and Trademark Office by Biblica, Inc.™

All emphases in Scripture quotations have been added by the authors.

Trade paperback ISBN: 978-1-4335-7124-4
ePub ISBN: 978-1-4335-7127-5
PDF ISBN: 978-1-4335-7125-1
Mobipocket ISBN: 978-1-4335-7125-1

Library of Congress Cataloging-in-Publication Data

Names: Marshall, Cheryl, 1970– author. | Newheiser, Caroline, 1958– author.
Title: When words matter most : speaking truth with grace into the lives of those you love / Cheryl Marshall and Caroline Newheiser.
Description: Wheaton, Illinois : Crossway, [2021] | Includes bibliographical references and index.
Identifiers: LCCN 2020054392 (print) | LCCN 2020054393 (ebook) | ISBN 9781433571244 (trade paperback) | ISBN 9781433571251 (pdf) | ISBN 9781433571251 (mobi) | ISBN 9781433571275 (epub)
Subjects: LCSH: Christian women—Religious life. | Conversation—Religious aspects—Christianity. | Interpersonal communication—Religious aspects—Christianity. | Truth—Religious aspects—Christianity.
Classification: LCC BV4527 .M2654 2021 (print) | LCC BV4527 (ebook) | DDC 248.8/43—dc23
LC record available at https://lccn.loc.gov/2020054392
LC ebook record available at https://lccn.loc.gov/2020054393

Crossway is a publishing ministry of Good News Publishers.

VP   30 29 28 27 26 25 24 23 22 21
15 14 13 12 11 10 9 8 7 6 5 4 3 2 1

Cheryl:
To my husband, Phillip, who has devoted
his life to speaking truth with grace.

Caroline:
To my husband, Jim, who exemplifies
incorporating Scripture into conversations.

Contents

Preface

WELCOME, READER, to a book about conversations. During the last few months of writing this book, personal conversations have taken on a new significance in our world. The COVID-19 pandemic has led to the shutdown of businesses, places of worship, schools, medical offices, and even parks and playgrounds. Government authorities have instructed us to wear masks, disinfect surfaces, wash our hands, stay in our homes, and keep a safe distance from others in public. As a result, the use of technology and social media to communicate has exploded as never before. Although unable to shake hands, give a hug, or even be in the same room together, as human beings we have still longed to connect with one another through words. Strangely, during the pandemic our longing to merely hear one another's voices has surpassed our desire to see one another's faces by digital means. A couple of months ago, an article in the *New York Times* explained:

> Phone calls have made a comeback in the pandemic. While the nation's biggest telecommunications providers prepared for a huge shift toward more internet use from home, what they didn't expect was an even greater surge in plain old voice calls, a medium

that had been going out of fashion for years. . . . "We've become a nation that calls like never before," said Jessica Rosenworcel, a commissioner at the Federal Communications Commission, the agency that oversees phone, television, and internet providers. "We are craving human voice."[1]

When Words Matter Most isn't about any and all conversations; it's about the conversations that matter most when fellow believers struggle spiritually—the conversations that encourage the worried, strengthen the weak, reprove the wayward, and comfort the weeping. There are moments in each of our lives when we crave a human voice, a voice that not only assures us we aren't alone but also tethers us to what is true. When burdened with fear or anxiety, weakness or inadequacy, sin or sorrow, we need our minds to be renewed, our hearts to be purified, and our souls to be strengthened. That is what God's word promises to do—and does do—for those who receive it by faith. Yes, we can read and meditate on Scripture by ourselves, but God, in his kindness and wisdom, has given us other believers to bring his word to bear in our lives. God has called each of us to speak his truth in love to one another, and that is what this book addresses—how to speak God's truth with grace into the lives of those you love, according to their need.

We (Cheryl and Caroline) met in 1995 at Grace Bible Church in Escondido, California, where Caroline's husband was a pastor and Cheryl's husband was a seminary intern. During those early years at the church, we were introduced to biblical counseling and learned the necessity and importance of using Scripture when caring for others. Although we have lived thousands of miles apart for many years now, the Lord has continued to teach both of us similar lessons about giving and receiving biblical wisdom and encouragement. Because we wanted this book to maintain a conversational tone, it made sense for us to write it in a single, unified voice, and yet what you will find on these pages reflects both of our thoughts and experiences. It's our desire to pass on to you what we have learned so that you too may be encouraged and equipped to speak God's truth in love.

Before we jump into chapter one, a few explanations are in order. First, we share many stories in this book about women who have been impacted by hearing and applying God's word to their lives. The women described are composites of those we have personally known; their names and some details of their stories have been changed to protect their privacy. Second, we have used feminine pronouns throughout the book, yet we realize that what is written here can also benefit you when speaking truth into the lives of male family members and friends. In addition, this book could be used by men to help other men. Third, the second half of the book, which contains several Scripture passages, is meant to be shared with those who are worried, weary, wayward, or weeping.

We are grateful that you have chosen to read *When Words Matter Most*. Although we wish we could sit with you over lunch and have a personal conversation about words, we trust that this book will help provide you with the understanding, confidence, and tools you need to speak truth with grace. Be encouraged! We have already prayed for you and the conversations you may have as a result of reading this book. This is our prayer for you even now:

Dear Lord,

Thank you for the woman who is reading this prayer. Thank you for giving her the desire to learn more about speaking truth with grace into the lives of those she loves. We ask that by reading this book, she will be encouraged to glorify you—to heed your call to speak your truth in love, to discern and respond to the spiritual needs of others, to comprehend your grace toward her, to be gracious when she speaks, and to trust your word to transform lives. You sent the word in the person of Jesus Christ. He is the Word of life, who alone can give her the wisdom and words to help others in their time of need. Please do that, Lord. We ask that your Spirit would teach and enable her to impact many lives with your truth, and we thank you in advance for what *you* will accomplish in and through her—to the praise of your glory. Amen.

Cheryl Marshall
Caroline Newheiser
June 20, 2021

PART 1

1

The Call to Speak

Speaking the truth in love, we are to grow up in
every way into him who is the head, into Christ.

EPHESIANS 4:15

"YOU KNOW WHAT YOUR PROBLEM IS? There's no one speaking truth into your life."

I (Cheryl) still remember where I was when my husband spoke those words. I was standing in our bedroom, still in my pajamas in the late afternoon, with tears streaming down my face. Since we'd relocated to Houston a few months earlier, it seemed that my tears had never stopped flowing. I'd lost count of our many moves during our fifteen years of marriage, and once again we'd left behind family, friends, and the familiar.

Without a new church home or any connections in the community, the isolation I felt was the last straw. I began to crumble under the crushing weight of the past few years. Money problems, homeschooling, twin babies, postpartum depression, and concerns for my extended family had taken their toll. My husband and three children needed me to be a wife and mom, but I had nothing left to give. I felt like a sponge squeezed in a tightening grip of sorrow—I was dry and depleted. As far as I was concerned, I was done with it all.

In the early mornings, I began reading the psalms. It was hard to pray or study the Bible as I had in the past, but I could underline. Huddled on a recliner in the corner of our bedroom, I began to mark the psalmists' phrases that resonated with my heart. I understood their complaints, and I clung to their convictions about who God is and what he's like. It was difficult to feast on the Scriptures, but at least I could taste the promises and praises others had written long ago. With gentle care, the Lord fed me.

He reminded me that I'm not alone. He reminded me that he's good and his word is true. He reminded me that I'm one of many throughout the ages who have hurt deeply and yet have found him faithful. I became convinced that he would lead me on a straight path out of the shadows, but I had no idea how much joy lay just around the bend. The Lord had prepared beautiful gifts in Houston that he would use to restore me. They would help me to see him, myself, and my life rightly once again.

My Truth Tellers

The first gift was Dede. This spunky mother of five, four of them by adoption, raced into my life with a contagious smile and a sassy twinkle in her eye. Dede immediately loved and welcomed me, as she does so many. We first met on a Sunday afternoon in early December, and within a couple of weeks she'd invited my family into her home for the holidays. With a generous and tenacious spirit, Dede found me wandering and took me in. Ever since then, her friendship has been a safe place for me, a place of transparency and unconditional love.

Liana was the second gift. Thoughtful, intentional, and compassionate, Liana is a natural-born teacher with a servant's heart. She was my fourth-grade son's tutor, and our friendship blossomed one summer as we sat on the steps of a community swimming pool discussing the finer points of theology while keeping an eye on our preschoolers. Little did I know the depth of spiritual encouragement and hours of iron-sharpening-iron conversation about doctrine and parenting that she would provide for years to come. Liana has proven to be a true and loyal friend.

The third gift was Rebecca. She's a pillar of faith, the kind of faith that's been forged in the fires of trial. As a divorced mother of two, she's endured many hardships resulting in genuine joy, a heart of wisdom, and a fruitful ministry to women in her local church. We met in our children's homeschool co-op, and our lives have been woven together ever since. Rebecca's example of trusting the Lord in every detail of her life has often convicted me of my lack of faith and at the same time spurred me on to trust him more.

Three different women. Three unique gifts from God. Three truth tellers who love the Lord and his word. He knew exactly what, or rather *whom*, I needed to help me persevere through those first rough months in Texas. Each of these women, with their God-given perspectives and personalities, unexpectedly entered my life and strengthened me with the love and words of God.

In my time of need, God helped me—he *loved* me—through the believing women he placed in my life. Through Dede, he gave me hope. Through Liana, he gave me strength. Through Rebecca, he gave me faith. What each of these women shared with me flowed out of their relationships with Christ and their understanding of the Scriptures. They naturally and freely spoke to me of God and his word. For many years now, we've experienced genuine Christian friendship rooted in our love for Christ. Countless conversations have made each of us more like Jesus as we've spoken his truth with grace.

When Words Matter Most

Have you ever been at a loss for words? Have you wondered what to say to someone who's going through a difficult season of life? Have you been aware of a spiritual need, but you haven't known how to address it? Maybe you've wanted to encourage someone with God's word, but you weren't sure where to turn in the Scriptures. Or maybe you've thought you should say something biblical and helpful, but you haven't known what to say. You're not alone. We have also felt that way, and we know many other women who have too.

We imagine you probably know someone who's struggling spiritually right now and needs to hear biblical truth. She needs a gracious, Christian woman to simply speak God's word into her life—to remind her of his promises, his character, and even his commands. She may be a friend who's hinted that her marriage is falling apart, or perhaps a coworker whose son recently passed away. She may be your teenage daughter who seems increasingly withdrawn, or your sister-in-law who's enduring a chronic illness. She may be the elderly woman who sits alone a couple rows in front of you each Sunday, or the young, frazzled mom on the back row who always arrives late. She may be your sister, cousin, or neighbor, who—for whatever reason—needs the word of God poured into her heart and life. Whoever she is, if you look and listen, you'll notice her. She's there.

We titled this book *When Words Matter Most* because we believe there are crucial moments in each of our lives when what is heard and believed makes all the difference in the world. When we're burdened with worry, weariness, sin, or sorrow, we have a choice to build our lives either on the rock of God's word or the sand of human wisdom. That choice has real consequences. Psalm 19:7–9 explains this so well. In these verses, King David describes God's word and its effects in the lives of those who receive it. Consider what he wrote:

> The law of the LORD is perfect,
>   reviving the soul;
> the testimony of the LORD is sure,
>   making wise the simple;
> the precepts of the LORD are right,
>   rejoicing the heart;
> the commandment of the LORD is pure,
>   enlightening the eyes;
> the fear of the LORD is clean,
>   enduring forever;
> the rules of the LORD are true,
>   and righteous altogether.

When words matter most, the very best we can do is speak the truth of God's word. This book is written *to encourage and equip you to speak truth with grace into the lives of those you love.* We'll share with you the lessons we've learned and are still learning about giving biblical wisdom, encouragement, and counsel. Now you might think, "Did you just say *counsel*? I'm not a counselor, and I don't plan on becoming one. Maybe this book isn't for me." Don't let the word *counsel* scare you! To give biblical counsel simply means *to wisely and graciously speak the truth of God's word to those you care about, according to their need.*

This book is for you if you're a Christian woman who wants to learn how to share Scripture in a helpful and meaningful way with other believers who are struggling spiritually in one way or another. You don't need to have a degree in biblical counseling or be a certified counselor to do that. While we believe that formal and informal training in biblical counseling is a good thing (and we do encourage it), it's not required in order for you to provide godly counsel. Three things are necessary to speak truth into the lives of those you love: a willingness to speak with them; an understanding of God's word; and an attitude of humility, grace, and love. Our hope is that *When Words Matter Most* will help you to see that you can do this and teach you how to do it well.

We're Not Alone

The Christian life isn't an isolated life. God never intended for us to walk alone. We were placed into his church. We each have a personal relationship with God through faith in Christ, but we're never to live spiritually independent of other believers. The Lord's design is for each of us to play a part in the spiritual well-being and growth of others.

Consider the word pictures given in the Scriptures to help us understand the significance of our relationships with one another in the church. God calls us a *family*. We have the same Father who loves us and the same brother who redeemed us. We're chosen and adopted, and together we inherit the eternal promises of God. We're the *body of Christ*. Jesus is our head, and he holds us together. We each have an important role to play as a member of his body so that it will function properly and grow strong. We're also called the *temple of God*. He's present within us, and we display his glory and gospel to one another and the world. We're built upon the firm foundation of his word and on Jesus our Savior, the perfect cornerstone.

These pictures remind us that we're never truly alone. Each of us is one of the millions whom Christ has redeemed. We're a part of the universal church of God—a family, a body, and a temple—that belongs, believes, worships, serves, grows, and perseveres together. God has given us to each other to help us become all he wants us to be in Christ. As the people of God, we must strengthen and encourage one another in the Lord, especially when the burdens we carry make the journey to our forever home long and difficult.

The Call to Speak

There are times when we desperately need to hear biblical wisdom and encouragement from someone who loves us. Sometimes those whom we love also need to hear *us* speak God's truth into *their* lives. We're sure you can name those close to you who are struggling spiritually or are experiencing difficult circumstances, and you feel burdened for them. God speaks through his word, and in his grace and goodness, he gives us opportunities to share his word with others and to point them to the Lord, who alone can meet their every need. There are certainly times for us to be quiet, to listen, and to pray. But there are also times for us to speak—to give *biblical* hope, encouragement, comfort, and correction.

In Ephesians 4:15 Paul writes, "Speaking the truth in love, we are to grow up in every way into him who is the head, into Christ." God wants us to speak what is true of him and his word to other believers for the purpose of promoting our mutual spiritual growth.

In a moment, we'll explain this in the context of Ephesians 4:11–16, but let's first see how Paul emphasizes this call to speak in other passages of Scripture:

> [Speak] . . . only such as is good for building up, as fits the occasion, that it may give grace to those who hear. (Eph. 4:29)

> Him we proclaim, warning everyone and teaching everyone with all wisdom, that we may present everyone mature in Christ. (Col. 1:28)

> Let the word of Christ dwell in you richly, teaching and admonishing one another in all wisdom. (Col. 3:16)

> Therefore encourage one another and build one another up, just as you are doing. (1 Thess. 5:11)

> We urge you, brothers, admonish the idle, encourage the fainthearted, help the weak, be patient with them all. (1 Thess. 5:14)

We glean two basic, yet vitally important, truths from these verses. First, we're commanded to speak with others to encourage their spiritual growth and maturity. Second, our words must be wise, true, and appropriate for the situation. We're to use our words like the woman in Proverbs 31:26 who honors the Lord: she "opens her mouth with wisdom, and the teaching of kindness is on her tongue." She impacts the lives of others because she's careful to speak wisely, faithfully, and appropriately to the need of her hearers.

Do you personally know this type of woman? Do you know a woman who obeys the call to encourage and instruct others with

God's word? These verses remind us of a mutual friend, Ana. I (Cheryl) met her at the church my husband and I attended soon after we were married. (It was the same church where Caroline and I first met.) Ana was several years older than me and already had school-aged children. At the time, she didn't teach a women's Bible study or formally mentor me, but I learned so much about speaking truth with grace simply by observing her. I watched her relationships and listened to her words; she loved and spoke well of her husband, and she carefully taught and disciplined her children. The occasional advice she gave me and the other young women in the church was always gentle and wise. What Ana said and how she spoke made such an impression on me that many times during the past twenty-plus years, I've silently asked myself in the middle of conversations, "What would Ana say? How would she respond? What biblical truth would Ana share, and how would she say it?"

Think about this: If God wants you to speak the truth in love—and he does—then he's also given you a platform to fulfill this calling. Just like Ana, you've been placed by God in a sphere of influence that is uniquely yours. No other believer has the exact same relationships that you do. The Lord has created a beautiful, intricate tapestry of relationships within his church, and you're a part of that grand design. Like a master weaver, the Lord has woven you into a particular place, at a particular time, for particular reasons, with particular people. It doesn't matter if your sphere of influence is small or large, seen or unseen. What matters is that you be faithful to God's calling to speak truth with grace right where you are with the people he has placed in your life. You, and your words, are significant and necessary for the building up of his church. Take a moment to think about your unique sphere of influence. Which names and faces come to mind?

Building Up the Body

As we continue to consider the importance of speaking God's truth to one another, let's look at this call in the context of Ephesians 4:11–16:

> He gave the apostles, the prophets, the evangelists, the shepherds and teachers, to equip the saints for the work of ministry, for building up the body of Christ, until we all attain to the unity of the faith and of the knowledge of the Son of God, to mature manhood, to the measure of the stature of the fullness of Christ, so that we may no longer be children, tossed to and fro by the waves and carried about by every wind of doctrine, by human cunning, by craftiness in deceitful schemes. Rather, *speaking the truth in love*, we are to grow up in every way into him who is the head, into Christ, from whom the whole body, joined and held together by every joint with which it is equipped, when each part is working properly, makes the body grow so that it builds itself up in love.

Notice that Paul first reminds us that God gives leaders to the church who faithfully and regularly preach and teach the word of God. These men equip us for "the work of ministry, for building up the body of Christ." "Building up" involves "developing another person's life through acts and words of love and encouragement."[1] By feeding us the word, our church leaders train us to build up the body of Christ, to serve and care for one another physically and spiritually. They teach us from the Scriptures how to be the hands, feet, and voice of Christ to one another.

Building up one another within the church isn't an activity reserved only for the "professionals," or those holding paid positions of service. Rather, it's God's purpose for each of us to pitch in and contribute to the spiritual health and edification of the body of Christ. We're gifted by the Lord to serve one another with the strength he provides and to speak his truth into each other's lives (1 Pet. 4:11). When we obediently serve and speak, Christ's church thrives and grows.

Three Goals

Several years ago, I (Caroline) decided to start running. In the beginning, it was a huge (and painful) accomplishment just to jog to the end of the block. Now, I can run miles at a time, and I've even completed several half marathons. When I train for a race, I set goals to run farther and faster, and those goals help me stay committed to my training schedule. I believe reaching those goals is worth the effort, even when my alarm goes off early in the morning so that I can beat the heat of the day.

In Ephesians 4:13, Paul gives us three goals to pursue for building up the body of Christ. Think of them as God's goals for your own personal relationships with other believers:

1. Unity of the faith
2. Knowledge of the Son of God
3. Christlike maturity

If you understand these goals and make them priorities in your relationships, they'll motivate you to continually encourage others in Christ, just like my running goals have helped me stay focused and committed to my training. To consider how you can begin pursuing these three God-given goals in your relationships, take a few minutes to thoughtfully answer the questions we've included at the end of each goal's explanation.

Goal #1: Unity of the Faith

Our first goal for building up one another is to be unified in our common faith. The next time you are in a worship service at your church, intentionally look around at your fellow worshipers. Take a few moments to notice their faces and expressions, especially during the singing and preaching of the word. Every unique countenance represents a different background, personality, and life experience, and yet in Christ we are all united. We are one body and share one Spirit, one hope, one Lord, one baptism, and one God (Eph. 4:4–6).

We also share one faith. In Ephesians 4:13, *faith* doesn't mean one's individual, subjective response toward God. Rather, in this passage *faith* means the doctrines and teachings of the Scriptures, especially in the gospel. As we help one another know, understand, and apply sound doctrine, God transforms our beliefs and behaviors to line up with his perfect word. When our minds are renewed and our lives are changed, we grow in peace and harmony with one another. To "attain to the unity of the faith," we must build up one another by reading, studying, and discussing Scripture together, encouraging one another to hold fast to the truth of God's word. Ask yourself:

- Is the unity of the faith (unity of doctrine) among believers important to me?
- Am I pursuing and growing in my knowledge of the Scriptures?
- How can I encourage other believers to also know, understand, and apply God's word?

Goal #2: Knowledge of the Son of God

The second goal of building up the body of Christ is for us to grow in experientially knowing him in a relationship of love, reverence, trust, and obedience. It goes without saying that to know Jesus means more than merely knowing facts about him and his life. Instead, to know Christ means to believe and receive him as the singular object of our faith and joy.

We build up the body of Christ by reminding one another who Christ is and what he's done for us. We strengthen one another with the realities and implications of his life, death, resurrection, ascension, and future return. We encourage one another to know and cherish our Savior above all else and to daily walk with him by faith. Like the apostle Paul, we "count all things to be loss in view of the surpassing value of knowing Christ Jesus" (Phil. 3:8 NASB). Ask yourself:

- Am I growing in my personal knowledge of Christ?
- Am I maturing in my relationship with him and helping others to do the same?
- How can my conversations help others to know, love, trust, and obey Jesus?

Goal #3: Christlike Maturity

Christlike maturity is the third goal for building up one another in the body of Christ. God places us in relationships with other believers to help us become more like his Son. Paul describes this goal as the pursuit of "mature manhood, to the measure of the stature of the fullness of Christ" (Eph. 4:13). Christ is the ultimate measure of spiritual and moral perfection, and as we continually submit our lives to him, we become more like him in our conduct and character. We all enter the family of God as spiritual infants, and from that time forward, our heavenly Father molds us into the image, or likeness, of his Son (Rom. 8:29).

God uses his Spirit, his word, and the circumstances of our lives to produce spiritual growth in us, and he also works through the influence of other Christians to help us forsake sin and pursue godliness. Each of us must do our part to "stir up one another to love and good works" (Heb. 10:24) and encourage one another to be imitators of Christ (1 Cor. 11:1). Ask yourself:

- Am I pursuing Christlikeness in my own life?
- Am I also concerned about godliness in the lives of other believers?
- How can I use my words to encourage Christlikeness in the lives of those I love?

A Firm Foundation

I (Cheryl) mentioned earlier that our family has moved several times over the years, and we've bought and sold a few homes along the way. Whenever we would look at a potential home to buy, one of the first things my husband and I would do was walk around the perimeter of the house to check the foundation. If we saw suspicious cracks or shifting in the foundation, then we'd get back in the car and immediately mark that house off our list, even if it had other features that we loved. We knew that a well-built home requires a strong and stable foundation. (My father was a structural engineer, and he taught me well!)

In the same way, these three goals for our relationships (the unity of the faith, the knowledge of God's Son, and Christlike maturity) must be built upon the strong foundation of God's word. It's the bedrock on which we build up one another. It's the truth we speak in love. The word—its teaching, correction, reproof, and training—equips us to live for God (2 Tim. 3:16–17). Paul explains in Ephesians 4:14 that as we build up one another in Christ, we will "no longer be children, tossed to and fro by the waves and carried about by every wind of doctrine, by human cunning, by craftiness in deceitful schemes." We will become spiritually strong and mature if we're rooted in the Scriptures. An old hymn says it well: "How firm a foundation, ye saints of the Lord, is laid for your faith in his excellent word!"[2]

Yes, This Means You

We now return to the call for you to speak truth into the lives of other believers. The Lord has given you a mandate to speak the truth in love:

> Rather, *speaking the truth in love*, we are to grow up in every way into him who is the head, into Christ, from whom the whole body, joined and held together by every joint with which it is equipped, when each part is working properly, makes the body grow so that it builds itself up in love. (Eph. 4:15–16)

Achieving God's good goals for your relationships requires *words*— specifically, your words communicating his word. As you begin to read this book, commit yourself *to speak wisely and graciously the truth of God's word to those you love, according to their need.* Be diligent to continually learn how to provide encouragement, comfort, and instruction from the Scriptures, and you'll become instrumental in helping others to grow in Christ. Although you may feel like a small, insignificant joint in a larger body, as you do your part, the church will grow and be strengthened in love.

Do you see the significant role you're to play in Christ's church? God certainly does! He didn't save you to live in spiritual isolation but to be involved and invested in the lives of others. God has prepared and placed you within the body of Christ to bless his people. The words of your mouth, speaking the truth of his word, will build up others in his Son. The body of Christ needs you, and God intends to use you for his special purposes right where you are.

REFLECTION QUESTIONS

1. Who has been used in your life to point you to Christ and his word? What has this person taught you? How has she encouraged you?

2. How is *counsel* defined in this chapter? What should "speaking the truth in love" look like? (See Eph. 4:15, 29; Col. 1:28; 3:16; 1 Thess. 5:11, 14.)

3. In Ephesians 4:13, what three goals are given for your relationships within the body of Christ? Explain each of them in your own words, and if you haven't already, answer the questions found in the "Three Goals" section of this chapter.

4. As you reflect on this chapter, what would you say to encourage a believer who feels alone in her walk with the Lord? What would you say to a believer who seems to be distancing herself from her church and other believers?

5. Do you know someone who's struggling spiritually and needs a genuine Christian friend? In what ways can you be that person for her? How can you build her up with God's word this coming week?

2

Those We Love

Admonish the unruly, encourage the fainthearted,
help the weak, be patient with everyone.

1 THESSALONIANS 5:14 NASB

IN 1972, "LEAN ON ME" was released by singer-songwriter Bill
Withers on his album *Still Bill*, and the song was an immediate success. I (Cheryl) first remember hearing "Lean on Me" in 1987, when
Club Nouveau released their version of the song. Again, it shot to the
top of the charts, winning a Grammy that year for best R&B song.
Even today the classic hit is ranked number 208 on "The 500 Greatest Songs of All Time" by *Rolling Stone*.[1] "Lean on Me" has a catchy
tune that's hard to forget, but it's the simple lyrics that make a lasting
impression. They speak to the reality that we all need someone to lean
on. We need an understanding friend who helps us keep going when
we're ready to give up and who shares the burdens we can't carry alone.

Thousands of years earlier, the author of Ecclesiastes realized his
need for the same kind of friend. He wrote, "Two are better than

one, because they have a good reward for their toil. For if they fall, one will lift up his fellow. But woe to him who is alone when he falls and has not another to lift him up!" (Eccles. 4:9–10). *Woe* is a strong word, meaning intense grief, misery, or affliction. To use the author's word-picture, God's people are colaborers who toil side by side. We till, plant, and reap in whatever fields the Lord has given us. But as we labor and toil, sometimes we stumble and fall. What woe if we fall alone! But what comfort and strength we receive when another believer lifts us up and helps us to keep going.

A Burdened Friend

When Kristine asked if she and I (Caroline) could get together to talk, she was extremely discouraged. Although she desired to live for God, Kristine repeatedly fell into old, sinful habits. She read her Bible and prayed sporadically, and when she resolved to be more disciplined in the word and prayer, her mind often wandered. Kristine's efforts seemed like a waste of time. She felt utterly defeated in her walk with the Lord.

Kristine's guilt about her stagnant spiritual growth was compounded as she saw others who seemed to have thriving, victorious Christian lives. She wondered what was wrong with her: "Am I even a Christian? Will I ever know the joy of my salvation? Why do I feel so stuck?" Kristine desperately wanted someone to talk to, someone who would not only listen but also understand and give encouragement.

Sometimes Kristine would send me texts telling me she was having a hard day, feeling emotionally and spiritually drained, and I'd reply with encouraging Bible verses and words of hope. Inevitably, Kristine would feel guilty about coming to me for help with the same problems time and time again, saying, "I'm so sorry, Caroline.

I don't want to burden you with my issues, but I'm still struggling." I'd reassure Kristine that we're meant to bear one another's burdens, and that I was not only available but also willing and eager to help.

Kristine needed someone to spiritually walk alongside her for many months. I listened to her concerns and asked a lot of questions so I could understand her better. I prayed for wisdom when I felt like I had none to give and pointed her to Christ and his word whenever I could. I began reminding Kristine of others long ago who'd also been discouraged, such as Elijah, Jeremiah, Jonah, and Job. These were real people with real struggles, and the Lord proved to them that he's always trustworthy and good. As we read about and discussed their lives, Kristine began to understand God's unwavering lovingkindness toward his people in the past and to realize that the Lord loves her in the same faithful way.

In time, Kristine's walk with the Lord took a significant turn. I could actually see it! She became strong in her faith and began sharing Bible verses with me for *my* encouragement. Kristine experienced a renewed confidence in the Lord's love for her and a joy in living each day for him. She told me that through our friendship, she learned that *Jesus* is the perfect friend—the friend of sinners—who did not come for the self-righteous but for the weak and needy. She saw him as her ultimate burden bearer who bore her sin on the cross, and now nothing could separate her from his love.

As I look back on those intense months of walking alongside Kristine, I'm thankful I could share the weight of her burdens through prayer and the encouragement of the Scriptures. Kristine is now a dear friend. She grew in her relationship with the Lord and so did I, as we learned to trust him together. I also learned more of what it means to be like Christ as I was challenged to patiently love Kristine and help carry her burdens.

Bear One Another's Burdens

Jesus commanded us to love one another as he has loved us. He said, "A new commandment I give to you, that you love one another; just as I have loved you, you also are to love one another. By this all people will know that you are my disciples, if you have love for one another" (John 13:34–35). As followers of Christ, we share a special relationship, or fellowship, with one another because we belong to him. The highest expression of the fellowship we share is love—a love that emulates the sacrificial, enduring love of Christ. One of the most significant ways we show that kind of love is by bearing one another's burdens. Galatians 6:2 says it plainly: "Bear one another's burdens, and so fulfill the law of Christ." Let's take a moment to carefully observe what this verse says and means, emphasizing one key word or phrase at a time:

- What does it mean *to bear*? It means to carry, but there's more to it than that. It means to carry with endurance. It's an expression of love that perseveres even in difficulty. And notice in Galatians 6:2 that it's a command!

- What is a *burden*? A burden is trouble that heavily weighs on someone. It's a load that's difficult to bear alone.

- What exactly is the *law of Christ*? It's the law of love. Christ's law, or command, is that we love one another as he has loved us (John 13:34–35; Gal. 5:13–14).

- And, finally, what does it mean that we *fulfill the law of Christ*? It simply means that when we love one another as he commands, we're obeying Jesus—we're doing exactly what he wants us to do.

In order to fulfill the law of Christ, our good intentions aren't enough. It's not the *thought* that counts. It's our *obedience* to Christ that makes a difference in the lives of those we love. We must not only be aware of the burdens that they carry; we must also be active in sharing the weight of those burdens. We may have our own concerns and troubles, but we are still responsible to help others with theirs. We like how one author put it: "Every believer is called to be one of God's bellhops, always ready to pick up someone else's baggage."[2]

Sometimes we help carry another's burden, or "baggage," in practical ways such as taking a meal to a new mother, running errands for a sick friend, giving gift cards to an unemployed family, or inviting a widow over for dinner. Often, though, to "bear one another's burdens" involves giving spiritual help to another person. Spiritual help isn't tangible. You can't touch it or put a price tag on it. Rather, it's communicated by words—the words we speak directly to the burdened and the words we pray to God on their behalf. We can provide spiritual help by listening (Prov. 18:13), sympathizing (Rom. 12:15), giving encouragement (Eph. 4:29), and interceding for others, praying that they'll receive mercy and grace in their time of need (Heb. 4:16). Isn't this how Jesus loves us even now? He listens, sympathizes, encourages, and intercedes for us. In these same ways, we can also love others and bear their burdens, and by doing so, we will obey Jesus.

Knowing Those We Love

After an exhausting day of attending college classes and studying, I (Cheryl) fell into bed early and was soon sound asleep as heavy rain poured outside my dormitory window. Around midnight, I was awakened by a loud banging on my door. Still half-asleep, I stumbled out of bed and opened the door to find a girl almost my age, rain-soaked from head to toe. She was frantically screaming and desperately attempting to tell me something, but in my sleepiness I couldn't recognize or understand her. After a moment of unsuccessfully trying to make sense of what she was saying, I flung my hands in the air and cried out, "I don't know who you are!"

"Aaaggghhh!" was all I heard as the frustrated girl turned and sprinted down the hall. Completely unaffected, I shut the door, staggered back to bed, and fell asleep without a second thought.

The next morning, after going to breakfast and attending a class, I walked across campus to the weekly chapel service. Not once did I think of the strange event from the night before. As the service began, my mind wandered to thoughts of my sister, Kathryn, who also attended the college. Suddenly, I remembered the girl banging on my door in the middle of the night. That raving lunatic had been my sister! Kathryn had needed me, but I hadn't recognized her. With a burst of panic, I scanned the chapel. There she was, safely sitting a few rows over from me.

After chapel, Kathryn told me that her car had stalled on a flooded road near campus during the previous night's storm. Unable to move the car or contact help, she ran almost a quarter mile in the pouring rain to find me. But once Kathryn found me and realized I was completely useless, she ran to get help elsewhere. Of course, I felt horrible. Now that years have passed, she still laughs when she tells the story and mimics my groggy, confused cry, "I don't know who you are!" And like a good sister, she makes me sound more ridiculous each time the story is told.

Unfortunately, this scenario often plays itself out in the reality of our relationships. Someone we love needs help bearing her burdens, but she isn't recognized or understood for who she is, so she doesn't receive the care appropriate for her need. We must seek to know and understand those we love and the burdens they carry so that our words will be meaningful, relevant, and helpful.

To begin to understand the needs of others, consider the burdens you have personally endured. Although we don't all experience the same circumstances, each of us will eventually carry the same kinds of burdens. Have you struggled with sin? Have you been wronged by the sin of another? Have you suffered consequences because of your own foolish choices or suffered the natural effects of living in a fallen world? At some point, all of us will struggle or suffer like those who are described in 1 Thessalonians 5:14: "We urge you, brethren, admonish the *unruly*, encourage the *fainthearted*, help the *weak*, be patient with everyone" (NASB).

In this short verse, we find three common difficulties that Christians experience: being unruly, growing fainthearted, and feeling weak. In addition, as we will see shortly, this passage teaches us how to respond to one another when we encounter these spiritual needs. Instead of neglecting these needs or being surprised by them in one another's lives, we must love one another enough to offer word-saturated strength, hope, and correction when words matter most.

Admonish the Unruly

The first instruction we find in 1 Thessalonians 5:14 is this: "Admonish the unruly." The term *unruly* was originally used in a military sense, describing someone who was out of step, out of line, or breaking rank.[3] Whether the soldier's unruliness came from apathy or defiance, he was considered insubordinate and in need of correction. Sometimes those we love may become "unruly," making choices which are clearly contrary to the Scriptures. Your friend might have confided in you that she's sleeping with her boyfriend.

A relative may regularly yell at her children and discipline them in anger. Your daughter may habitually gossip about other kids at school. A coworker might stop attending church altogether. These choices are sin issues in direct disobedience to God's word.

When a believer is characteristically and persistently disobedient, we're to admonish her. To *admonish* literally means to "put in mind."[4] With gentleness, we're to put in her mind an understanding that her choices are in opposition to the Lord and that she must turn from her sin to obey Christ. We're to remind and instruct her from the Scriptures about her sin, warn her about the consequences that may result from her choices, and help restore her relationship with God and others.

These admonishments, or reproofs, are never to be given with a harsh or critical spirit but with a compassionate and genuine concern like Paul had for the Ephesian believers. Before leaving Ephesus, he reminded them that for three years he had not ceased to "admonish every one with tears" (Acts 20:31). It's not easy to address sin in another person's life, but when you need to, the Lord will provide you with wisdom and grace to speak truth in love to the unruly.

Encourage the Fainthearted

Yesterday morning, after finishing the breakfast dishes, I (Cheryl) was eager to start crossing items off my long to-do list. Because I expected a friend to stop by around noon for a quick visit and then I had to teach piano lessons in the afternoon, there were only a few short hours for me to get things done. The Lord had other plans.

Somehow, I got into a conversation with my teenage son that I couldn't cut short. I've learned that when one of my children starts to open up, I need to stop and embrace the moment while it lasts.

My boy was discouraged and needed me, but even more, he needed to hear God's truth. His heart was too heavy to carry alone, so we carried it together. By the end of our hour-long conversation, I couldn't have cared less about the pressures of my daily responsibilities. I had done what God wanted me to do.

In 1 Thessalonians 5:14 we're instructed to "encourage the fainthearted." The fainthearted are the discouraged, those who are "little-spirited" or small-souled.[5] They feel small compared to the burdens they carry and the obstacles they face. They may be overwhelmed, anxious, and fearful, lacking strength and courage to persevere.

Your fainthearted friend might feel like Caroline's friend Kristine, who was burdened by her lack of spiritual discipline and growth in the Lord. She may feel like Jessica, an exhausted mother of small children, who can't see beyond the sleepless nights and piles of laundry. She may be like Diane, a widow who misses her husband terribly and now must count every dollar. Or perhaps she feels like my (Cheryl's) son, whose teenage challenges seemed insurmountable. Discouragement fills their hearts, and they need someone who will not only listen to their sorrows but also build up their faith.

The fainthearted person isn't to be admonished or rebuked. Instead, she's to be encouraged. The word translated here as *encourage* can also mean "to soothe, console."[6] With a gentle spirit, come alongside the fainthearted with words of comfort, peace, and courage. Console her heart and reinforce her faith with reminders of God's faithful character and promises that have personally helped you in your own time of need. Don't hesitate to encourage her with biblical truth that she may already know. In times of trouble, we all need constant reminders of what we know is true about God, just like the psalmist who repeatedly asked himself, "Why are you cast down, O my soul, and why are you in turmoil within me?" Each time, he reassured his own faint heart with the same words of encouragement: "Hope in God; for I shall again praise him, my salvation and my God" (Ps. 42:5, 11; 43:5).

Help the Weak

Our culture seems to be obsessed with strength and self-sufficiency. Weakness must be overcome at all costs, and if it's not, then it's justified, ignored, or hidden. We can feel the pressure to "have it all together," but we often fall short. When we're weak, we need the loving support of other believers who are strong. The Anglican bishop J. C. Ryle once tenderly observed: "Our Lord has many weak children in his family, many dull pupils in his school, many raw soldiers in his army, many lame sheep in his flock. Yet he bears with them all, and casts none away. Happy is that Christian who has learned to do likewise with his brethren."[7]

In 1 Thessalonians 5:14 we're reminded how to respond to one another when we experience the familiar burden of weakness: we're simply told to "help the weak." The weak person in this context is feeble and without strength, either spiritually or morally.[8] She might be unsteady in her faith, doubting the word of God or her salvation. For example, Olivia suffers from a debilitating disease and questions whether God truly loves her. Sandy struggles to understand her heart-wrenching childhood, wondering how God can be both sovereign and good. Karen fears she might not be a Christian because she can't meet the outward expectations of her church culture.

On the other hand, someone may be morally weak. Perhaps she's ignorant of what the Scriptures teach or lacks conviction and fortitude to obey the Lord. Angela might be a new believer and not know God's will for purity in her relationships. Carrie may struggle with knowing how to respect her husband and control her excessive spending habits. Amber might be turning to overeating, substance abuse, or pornography to escape the pressures in her life. Regardless of your loved one's weakness, God has placed you in her life to help.

The word translated in this verse as *help* can indicate holding firmly to someone or something, and it also can imply supporting another.[9] When someone you love runs headlong toward a dangerous cliff of doubt, foolishness, or sin, quickly take hold of her and pull with all your God-given strength to keep her from falling. Make every effort to help her know and trust God's word and provide her with ongoing accountability as she gains solid footing in her walk with the Lord. Helping the weak requires sacrificial, personal involvement. She'll need your patience, friendship, and persistent application of biblical truth to her life in order to become strong in faith and obedience to Christ.

The Unbelievers We Love

We've seen in 1 Thessalonians 5:14 three types of burdens believers carry and how we can help them, but it's likely you also know and love an *unbeliever* who's burdened with sin or suffering. You may wonder, "How can I speak truth into her life? How can I offer her wisdom and hope from the Scriptures if she doesn't believe God or his word? How can I help bear her burdens?" To begin, bear her burdens just like you would those of believers:

- Help meet her physical needs. Love and serve her, sacrificially sharing your time, friendship, and resources (Heb. 13:16).

- Pray for her and her concerns. Pray in faith, knowing our heavenly Father is good and merciful to all his creatures (Ps. 145:9).

- Offer biblical wisdom. If she'll listen, share biblical truth and principles that apply to her circumstances. God's ways are always best and beneficial to those who put them into practice (Prov. 3:1–2).

But then, and most importantly, address the unbeliever's greatest need—to be reconciled to God through Christ. Sin has separated her from God, and because of her sin she remains under his judgment (Rom. 2:2; 3:23). All her other burdens are light when compared to the burden of her sin. Christ is her only hope for being relieved of this weight, and God has sent you to her with an urgent message to be reconciled to him:

> Christ reconciled us to himself and gave us the ministry of reconciliation; that is, in Christ God was reconciling the world to himself, not counting their trespasses against them, and entrusting to us the message of reconciliation. Therefore, we are ambassadors for Christ, God making his appeal through us. We implore you on behalf of Christ, be reconciled to God. (2 Cor. 5:18–20)

You are Christ's ambassador to the unbeliever whose burdens you help carry. God has placed you in her life to provide tangible help and to lovingly speak on his behalf: "Be reconciled to God" (2 Cor. 5:20). Share with her the message of reconciliation, that the only way to have peace with God is through personal faith in Jesus Christ, who died and rose again on our behalf:

God shows his love for us in that while we were still sinners, Christ died for us. Since, therefore, we have now been justified by his blood, much more shall we be saved by him from the wrath of God. For if while we were enemies we were reconciled to God by the death of his Son, much more, now that we are reconciled, shall we be saved by his life. More than that, we also rejoice in God through our Lord Jesus Christ, through whom we have now received reconciliation. (Rom. 5:8–11)

But you might then wonder, "What if the unbeliever I love doesn't respond in faith to Christ? Can Scripture help someone who isn't reconciled to God? Can I still use God's word when talking with someone about her problems, even though she denies Christ?" Absolutely! And here's why:

1. *Jesus opens minds to understand the Scriptures* (Luke 24:45; Acts 16:14). We can confidently share God's word with unbelievers, knowing that "faith comes from hearing, and hearing through the word of Christ" (Rom. 10:17). Perhaps God will use your word-saturated counsel to draw someone to himself. In fact, biblical truth often becomes clear to those who are burdened by physical and spiritual needs. As the psalmist said, "It is good for me that I was afflicted, that I might learn your statutes" (Ps. 119:71).

2. *Jesus commands us to make disciples, which includes teaching others what he's taught us* (Matt. 28:19–20). Have you ever thought of yourself as a teacher and your sphere of influence as your classroom? What are you teaching—God's wisdom or your own? What you do say and don't say to unbelievers in their time of need will teach them something. If you want to help them

understand themselves, their circumstances, and the Lord rightly, explain what God says in his word. When you have an opening to share what he's taught you from the Scriptures, don't let that opportunity pass you by.

3. *Jesus is the ultimate wisdom unbelievers need* (1 Cor. 1:30–31). It may be tempting to simply give unbelievers advice to help their lives run more smoothly, but offering principles for life without the hope and power of the gospel won't give them relief from their heaviest burden—the burden of sin and its condemnation. Beware of providing unbelievers with only temporary solutions that ignore the spiritual realities in their lives. Instead, direct them to Christ, the wisdom from God for salvation. In him, they will find wisdom and knowledge for all of life (Col. 2:3).

We and those we love, both believers and unbelievers, need Jesus, his gospel, and his word. Jesus is the ultimate burden-bearer, and he will never disappoint us (Rom. 10:11). Only in Christ do we find the help and grace that we *all* need.

REFLECTION QUESTIONS

---

1. Read Galatians 6:1–4. What do these verses tell you about the who, how, and why of carrying one another's burdens? How does this expand your understanding of how to love other believers?

2. In 1 Thessalonians 5:14, what are three common types of burdens people may carry? Explain in your own words how God wants you to respond to each of them.

46

3. Think of someone you know who's burdened in one of the ways listed in 1 Thessalonians 5:14. What burden does she carry, and how can you specifically help carry that burden? What Scripture passages have been meaningful in your own life that you could share with her to help meet her spiritual need?

4. What is the greatest need of the unbeliever? What are some practical ways you can love her? Which of the three points about Jesus from the end of this chapter gives you courage to share God's word with her, and why?

5. Spend some time praying for those you love who are unruly, faint-hearted, weak, or unbelieving. Select one of the following prayers of Paul to guide your prayer: Ephesians 1:16–19 or Ephesians 3:14–19. Ask the Lord for wisdom and opportunities to share with them biblical truth that's appropriate for their spiritual needs.

3

The Greater Grace

For from his fullness we have all received, grace upon grace.

JOHN 1:16

WHEN MY OLDEST SON was a small child, he'd ask me (Cheryl) to sing a hymn he liked to call "Grace, Grace" as I tucked him into bed at night. I first began singing the song to him when he was a baby because I wanted to plant deep in his little heart the truth that God's grace is greater than all our sin. I can't count the number of times I sang these words:

Marvelous grace of our loving Lord,
Grace that exceeds our sin and our guilt!
Yonder on Calvary's mount outpoured,
There where the blood of the Lamb was spilled.

Grace, grace, God's grace,
Grace that will pardon and cleanse within;

Grace, grace, God's grace,
Grace that is greater than all our sin![1]

Many nights, tears ran down my face as I sang and knelt beside
my son's bed. I cried over my own sinfulness of the day, usually
because I had responded to him with anger instead of kindness
and impatience instead of grace. As a young mother, I was learning the lesson that if what I speak is true and yet *without* grace,
then my words still fall short of honoring God and loving others.
This verse became very instructive to me: "Let no corrupting talk
come out of your mouths, but only such as is good for building
up, as fits the occasion, that it may give grace to those who hear"
(Eph. 4:29).

The Lord taught me another important lesson about my words
during those early years of motherhood: even if I do speak with
grace, my words don't guarantee an outcome. I remember many
days spent addressing my son's heart issues, yet he'd still be stubbornly unrepentant at bedtime. As I'd turn out the lights and sadly
leave his room, God was teaching me to trust *his* grace. I learned
I don't have the power to change another person's heart, but God
does. I can't control how or when someone responds to the Scriptures, but God can. I'm not the one who saves and sanctifies, but
God is. He may choose to use me as a godly influence in the lives
of those I love, but the transforming work is his alone. No matter
how gracious I am, his grace is always greater than mine.

Grace Greater than Mine

I (Cheryl) was reminded of God's life-changing grace in a recent
conversation with Theresa, a friend from church. Theresa and her
husband became Christians when their children were teenagers and

getting into some serious trouble. Although Theresa's children are still unbelievers, they've matured into young adults and are now making better decisions. Her relationships with them, however, are still strained, and communication remains difficult.

Theresa and I usually meet for lunch once every few weeks to talk about the latest challenges in her family and Scripture passages that apply to her concerns. Several months ago, I was trying to help Theresa see that she often blamed her children for the angry ways she responded to them, but she couldn't see it. Knowing that the Lord has been very patient with me and my shortcomings, I wanted to be patient with Theresa too. I began praying that the Lord would work in her heart and teach her whatever he wanted her to learn.

I was pleasantly surprised by Theresa's excitement when we met together a few weeks ago. She couldn't wait to tell me about an audio sermon of Luke 6:41–45 she had listened to the previous week. In that passage, Jesus taught that we must humbly deal with our own sin before we address sin in others. She explained how deceived she'd been about her own angry responses to her children and that she couldn't continue blaming them for her behavior. She finally understood that her choices reflected the attitudes in her own heart. As she humbled herself before the Lord, she was learning to respond to others with humility. Theresa now had great hope for improving her relationships with her children because, as she explained, "God is changing *my* heart!"

Listening to that sermon was a turning point for Theresa. What the Spirit taught her continues to positively impact how she relates to her children, and it's certainly not because of anything I said. It's because of God's grace. He was gracious to work in her life in his own way and in his own time.

Grace Has Appeared

Speaking truth with grace begins with receiving and knowing the grace of God in our own lives. Without understanding God's grace to us through Christ, we're unable to extend God-honoring grace to others through our words. Our personal knowledge of his lovingkindness toward us is foundational for knowing how to communicate with love. Our ability to enter another's life with a disposition of grace is built upon our experience and appreciation of God's marvelous grace toward us.

In Colossians 4:6 Paul instructs us, "Let your speech always be gracious." Gracious words are considerate words, conveying a genuine attitude of love and kindness. They promote the well-being and good of others: "Gracious words are like a honeycomb, sweetness to the soul and health to the body" (Prov. 16:24). If we desire to speak truth into the lives of those we love, our words must be expressions of grace.

Jesus, the Word who became flesh, is the ultimate expression of God's grace toward us. He's the embodiment of the Father's infinite love, and in him we receive every spiritual blessing from the hand of God: "For from his fullness we have all received, grace upon grace" (John 1:16). The apostle Paul actually refers to Jesus as "the grace of God" when he writes:

> *The grace of God has appeared*, bringing salvation for all people, training us to renounce ungodliness and worldly passions, and to live self-controlled, upright, and godly lives in the present age, waiting for our blessed hope, the appearing of the glory of our great God and Savior Jesus Christ, who gave himself for us to redeem us from all lawlessness and to purify for himself a people for his own possession who are zealous for good works. (Titus 2:11–14)

These verses reveal the outpouring of God's abundant grace to us in Christ. Because of him, we have been saved, are being sanctified, and will one day be glorified. In this chapter, we'll explore these gifts of God's marvelous grace and consider how they teach and enable us to speak with grace.

The Grace That Saves

The grace of God has appeared, bringing salvation for all people . . . to redeem us from all lawlessness. (Titus 2:11, 14)

At just the right time in history, Christ came into the world to redeem us from our sin and to reconcile us to God: "But when the fullness of time had come, God sent forth his Son, born of woman, born under the law, to redeem those who were under the law, so that we might receive adoption as sons" (Gal. 4:4–5). We failed to meet the demands of God's law, but Jesus was victorious and accomplished all that our salvation requires. Anything we think, say, or do that's contrary to God's word is sin, and the punishment we deserve is not only physical death but also spiritual death away from his presence forever (Rom. 3:23; 6:23). We're guilty before the law, and that's a verdict we can't overturn ourselves. And yet God's grace is greater than all our sin.

To understand the grace that brings us salvation, imagine yourself standing before a judge in a courtroom. You've broken the law, and the penalty amounts to a fine so enormous you could never earn or borrow enough money to pay it. As the judge is about to pronounce you guilty, someone else suddenly steps between you and the judge. It's not a friend or a family member. It's not someone who owes you a favor. No, it's a stranger you've never met before, but he somehow knows that you're guilty of the crime and that you're penniless. This person has never broken the law. On the contrary, he's done all that the law requires. This unexpected visitor addresses the judge, saying he'll bear your sentence of guilt, and he pays your fine in full. The court records your crime as his offense and credits his perfect law keeping to you. The judge strikes his gavel and declares the verdict. Completely amazed, you leave the courtroom justified!

To be *justified* means to be declared forgiven of your sin and righteous in God's sight because of Jesus's death on your behalf. You stood before God rightly condemned for your sin, but Jesus willingly offered himself as your substitute on the cross and received the punishment you deserve. Because Jesus completely paid your debt, your sin is no longer held against you. You're fully forgiven: "In him we have redemption through his blood, the forgiveness of our trespasses, according to the riches of *his grace*" (Eph. 1:7).

Not only did Jesus die in your place; he also lived a sinless life so that his righteousness becomes yours. You could never perfectly obey God, but Jesus did. As your sin was credited to him, his complete obedience was credited to you (2 Cor. 5:21). Your filthy robe of sin was removed and replaced with the gleaming robe of Jesus's righteousness: "I will greatly rejoice in the LORD; my soul shall exult in my God, for he has clothed me with the garments of salvation; he has covered me with the robe of righteousness" (Isa. 61:10).

God's saving grace toward you isn't a result of your personal merit or efforts, "for by *grace* you have been saved through faith. And this is not your own doing; it is *the gift of God*, not a result of works" (Eph. 2:8–9). You're justified because of Christ's work and worth, not your own. Your salvation is wholly by his bountiful grace, and you simply receive it by faith, with humility, gratitude, and great joy.

Understanding God's grace in our salvation will shape our priorities as we bear one another's burdens. Meeting others' physical and material needs is important, but the primary spiritual need—a genuine relationship with God through Christ—will become an overarching priority in our relationships. When we've experienced saving grace, we'll desire that others also know Christ by faith and be strengthened in his love. Paul expresses this priority in his prayer for the Ephesian believers:

> For this reason I bow my knees before the Father, . . . that according to the riches of his glory he may grant you to be strengthened with power through his Spirit in your inner being, *so that Christ may dwell in your hearts through faith—that you, being rooted and grounded in love, may have strength . . . to know the love of Christ that surpasses knowledge.* (Eph. 3:14, 16–19)

We've seen a common struggle among some who profess faith in Christ: they find it hard to believe that God truly loves and accepts them. We've heard sentiments such as "I'm not good enough," "I've been too bad," or "If you only knew what I've done." They dwell on personal sins that they believe make it difficult, or impossible, for God to fully forgive and love them. Some are so laden with guilt that they feel like second-rate Christians who can't worship or serve the Lord. In addition, they may think that there's something more they must do to appease God or be received by him.

Maybe you know a believer like this, burdened by past or present sin, who needs the encouragement of knowing that her salvation is complete and secure in Christ. Remind her that God's love for her is not based on her performance but on the perfect life and sacrifice of Christ. She's been justified—forgiven and declared righteous—by his grace. So if she sins, speak of God's forgiveness. If she fails, speak of God's mercy. If she doubts, speak of God's faithfulness. If she suffers, speak of God's lovingkindness. And if she hurts or offends you, remember that as God has been gracious to you in your salvation, you must also be gracious to her—especially when you speak.

The Grace That Sanctifies

The grace of God has appeared, . . . training us to renounce ungodliness and worldly passions, and to live self-controlled, upright, and godly lives. (Titus 2:11–12)

The Billy Graham Library is about a thirty-minute car ride from my (Caroline's) home, and it's become a favorite site for my husband and me to visit. I especially enjoy walking through the peaceful Memorial Prayer Garden located on the library grounds. There you'll find the simple burial site for Billy Graham and his wife, Ruth Bell Graham. These words are engraved on Mrs. Graham's gravestone: "End of construction—Thank you for your patience." A nearby plaque explains that Mrs. Graham once saw a sign with those words along the side of a road and requested they be placed on her grave. Her husband later explained:

> While we found the humor enlightening, we appreciated the truth she conveyed through those few words. Every human being is under construction from conception to death. Each life is made up of mistakes and learning, waiting and growing, practicing patience and being persistent. At the end of construction—death—we have completed the process.[2]

It's often said that Jesus meets us where we are. That's true, but it's not the whole story. He doesn't leave us where he finds us. We've seen in Titus 2 that Jesus came to save us, and now we see that he also came to change us—to train us to forsake sin and to pursue godliness (Titus 2:12). We were *declared* righteous when we were justified, but we *become* righteous as we're sanctified. Both are a work of God's grace in our lives.

Sanctification is "a progressive work of God and man that makes us more and more free from sin and like Christ in our actual lives."[3] It's the process of being conformed to Christ in our desires, thoughts, words, and actions. It's our spiritual growth as we become more like Jesus in character and conduct. He's the master builder, and we're under construction. By his grace at work in us, we're being built into his image.

Imagine you're watching one of the many popular television reality shows that follows a home's renovation process. First, the buyers choose and purchase an older, rundown house with all its problems and quirks. Experts then help the new owners cast a vision for their home and draw up plans for repairs and updates to suit their purposes and personalities. Next, it's time for the hard work of the actual remodeling. Out with the old and in with the new.

After several weeks, the day arrives for the "big reveal." All work on the house is complete, down to the smallest creative detail. Cameras roll as the excited homeowners see the finished project for the first time, and with lots of "oohs" and "aahs" they tour the house, surprised by all the stunning changes. The once rundown house is now a beautiful home—*their* beautiful home—and the transformation is amazing. The results are better than they had ever dreamed!

Just like the renovation of a home takes time, your ongoing sanctification is a long-term pursuit of becoming like Christ. God is working in you to make you more like his Son in faith and obedience, and he won't stop until the work is complete and you see him face to face (1 John 3:2). In Christ, you've been set free from sin's power to control you, yet a struggle against sin still remains within you. The Spirit of God teaches and enables you to say no to sin and yes to the things of God. Instead of being enslaved to sin, you're now free to follow and honor Christ (Rom. 6:17–18).

Not only is the Lord working in you to conform you to his image; you're also commanded to participate in your sanctification: "Work out your own salvation with fear and trembling, for it is God who works in you, both to will and to work for his good pleasure" (Phil. 2:12–13). This doesn't mean that you work to earn your salvation—Jesus already did that. Rather, you obey God as an outworking of the salvation you've already received by faith. As he works in you to change your desires and behavior to glorify him, you are to forsake sin and actively pursue obedience to his word.

It's the grace of Christ that trains you to pursue godliness and purifies you to live for him (Titus 2:12, 14). Like a master craftsman who uses various tools to renovate an old house into a family's dream home, the Lord uses various "tools" to bring you to spiritual maturity: his word, prayer, suffering, the ordinances and ministries of the church, and encouragement from other believers. To grow in Christlikeness, receive these provisions as gifts of God's sanctifying grace. With them he will "equip you with everything good that you may do his will, working in us that which is pleasing in his sight, through Jesus Christ" (Heb. 13:21).[4]

In heaven, when you are fully and forever sanctified, your joy will be indescribable. Can you imagine no more "put[ting] to death the deeds of the body" (Rom. 8:13)? At last, you'll be perfectly righteous in body and soul. You'll be entirely free from the presence of sin. You'll be made holy like the Lord. The final result of your sanctification will be beyond anything you could ask or think: "And I am sure of this, that he who began a good work in you will bring it to completion at the day of Jesus Christ" (Phil. 1:6). Your construction will be complete.[5]

Understanding God's gracious work in our own sanctification teaches and motivates us to speak with patience to others who are also being sanctified. We know from Scripture and personal experience that our sanctification is a progressive, lifelong journey. Sometimes we grow by leaps and bounds, and sometimes we take baby steps. Sometimes we may feel that we're stuck in one place, not making much progress at all. But God is always patient with us as we're being conformed to the image of his Son day by day:

> The LORD is merciful and gracious,
> slow to anger and abounding in steadfast love. . . .
> He does not deal with us according to our sins,
> nor repay us according to our iniquities. . . .
> As a father shows compassion to his children,
> so the LORD shows compassion to those who fear him.
> For he knows our frame;
> he remembers that we are dust. (Ps. 103:8, 10, 13–14)

Like a compassionate father, the Lord knows our spiritual weakness and immaturity, but he doesn't treat us as our sins deserve. As he is patient with us, so also must we be longsuffering with the spiritual shortcomings and struggles of others. Instead of attacking or giving up on those who struggle with sin, we must extend an attitude of humility that communicates, "I sin, just as you do too. Neither of us is perfect, but our Savior is, and he's changing us to become more like him. God will give us the grace we both need to grow in faith and obedience, and we can trust him for that together."

The apostle Paul provides an endearing example of patience that is worth following. He wrote to the Thessalonian Christians:

> We were gentle among you, like a nursing mother taking care of her own children. . . . You are witnesses, and God also, how holy and righteous and blameless was our conduct toward you believers. For you know how, like a father with his children, we exhorted each one of you and encouraged you and charged you to walk in a manner worthy of God. (1 Thess. 2:7, 10–12)

As with Paul, being patient with those you love doesn't mean you never say the hard things that they may need to hear. Instead, it means that when you do encourage or admonish others to walk in a manner worthy of God, you speak with the gentleness of a devoted mother and the heartfelt concern of a loving father. Your love for others will be measured by the patience—and grace—with which you speak (1 Cor. 13:4).

The Grace That Glorifies

> The grace of God has appeared, . . . [and now we are] waiting for our blessed hope, the appearing of the glory of our great God and Savior Jesus Christ. (Titus 2:11–13)

In Christ we're showered with "grace upon grace" (John 1:16). Like our justification and sanctification, our glorification is also a gift of God. It's the final link in the chain of grace that cannot be broken: "For those whom he foreknew he also predestined to be conformed to the image of his Son. . . . And those whom he predestined he also called, and those whom he called he also justified, and those whom he justified he also glorified" (Rom. 8:29–30). Our future glory is a sure promise of God.

Jesus is our blessed hope of eternal life. When Christ returns, he'll give us glorified, resurrected bodies: "Our citizenship is in heaven, and from it we await a Savior, the Lord Jesus Christ, who will transform our lowly body to be like his glorious body" (Phil. 3:20–21). When he appears, our glorification will be

> the final step in the application of redemption. It will happen when Christ returns and raises from the dead the bodies of all believers for all time who have died, and reunites them with their souls, and changes the bodies of all believers who remain alive, thereby giving all believers at the same time perfect resurrection bodies like his own.[6]

The hope of our future glory in Christ recently came into sharper focus for me (Cheryl). A couple of weeks ago, my close friend's teenage son unexpectedly passed away. Because of God's eternal promises, my friend knows she'll see her son again in heaven, but here and now the pain is excruciating. The sting of her son's death is sharp, yet she doesn't grieve like those without hope. In the midst of her deep sorrow, she's looking with the eyes of faith to her Savior, who gives victory over death and will clothe his people with resurrection bodies to enjoy him and the gifts of his grace forever (1 Cor. 15:51–58).

Like children who excitedly anticipate the joys and surprises of Christmas morning, we eagerly await our future glory, yet we can't imagine the fullness of that experience: "No eye has seen, nor ear heard, nor the heart of man imagined, what God has prepared for those who love him" (1 Cor. 2:9). But he does give us glimpses in his word of the everlasting graces that will be ours in heaven:

1. Eternal life with Christ:

I am the resurrection and the life. Whoever believes in me, though he die, yet shall he live, and everyone who lives and believes in me shall never die. (John 11:25–26)

2. A heavenly home:

In my Father's house are many rooms. . . . And if I go and prepare a place for you, I will come again and will take you to myself, that where I am you may be also. (John 14:2–3)

3. Freedom from sin:

Beloved, we are God's children now, and what we will be has not yet appeared; but we know that when he appears we shall be like him, because we shall see him as he is. (1 John 3:2)

4. Deliverance from sorrow and pain:

He will wipe away every tear from their eyes, and death shall be no more, neither shall there be mourning, nor crying, nor pain anymore, for the former things have passed away. (Rev. 21:4)

5. Rewards for service:

Each one's work will become manifest, for the Day will disclose it. . . . If the work that anyone has built on the foundation survives, he will receive a reward. (1 Cor. 3:13–14)

6. Authority to reign with Christ:

For you [Christ] were slain, and by your blood you ransomed people for God from every tribe and language and people and nation . . . and they shall reign on the earth. (Rev. 5:9–10)

These eternal gifts are ours because of Christ. His life, death, and resurrection secured our future glory: "When Christ who is your life appears [again], then you also will appear with him in glory" (Col. 3:4). In heaven, we'll enjoy these good gifts, but our greatest joy will be the presence of God's greatest grace—Christ himself: "*You* make known to me the path of life; in *your* presence there is fullness of joy; at *your* right hand are pleasures forevermore" (Ps. 16:11).

Having such an understanding of God's grace toward us in our glorification provides us with an eternal perspective when we speak truth into the lives of those we love. Because we realize this world is temporary and our future glory is eternal, we persevere with hope in our suffering, and we encourage others to do the same. There's no sugarcoating it—life is hard—yet when we remember God's future graces, we can help one another endure all hardship knowing that there is eternal glory still to come (2 Cor. 4:17).

One way to speak with grace in light of future glory is to saturate the encouragement you give to others with the comforting and eternal perspectives found in Hebrews 12. As we look to Jesus, we're reminded that the weight of our current troubles and sorrows doesn't compare to the eternal joy that will be ours in the presence of God (Heb. 12:2). As we consider the severity of all that our Savior suffered and endured, we can persevere through our own suffering with patience and hope (Heb. 12:3). When we're disciplined by the Lord, we can trust that his correction and training is for our good, to make us holy (Heb. 12:10). And knowing that we'll live forever with Christ in his unshakable kingdom, we can refuse to be shaken *today*. Rather, we can worship God on this side of glory with hearts full of gratitude, reverence, and awe (Heb. 12:28).

As you grow in understanding and appreciating the grace of God in your own life—especially as you meditate on his grace in your salvation, sanctification, and glorification—your speech will become more grace-filled. Your words will become more loving, and you will find yourself speaking freely of the grace of God. Every day holds opportunities for you to encourage others with the realities of God's lovingkindness toward them in Christ. As you speak of him and his word, always speak with grace.

REFLECTION QUESTIONS

1. Read Ephesians 4:29–32 and list all the ways your speech can "give grace to those who hear," according to these verses. Who in your life has spoken to you with grace, and how?

2. Have you personally experienced the saving grace of God? What does justification mean, and how is someone justified? How might understanding saving grace impact how you speak with others?

3. What is sanctification, and how does it differ from your initial salvation? How might understanding biblical sanctification impact how you speak with others?

4. What are the future graces that await all glorified believers in heaven? Which of these are the most meaningful to you, and why? How might your understanding of biblical glorification impact how you speak with others?

5. Read Titus 2:11–14 and list all that you learn about the grace of God. As you meditate on these verses, take a few minutes to

thank God for his abundant grace toward you in Christ. Next, pray for someone you know who needs to be encouraged with a reminder of God's grace in her life. What can you share with her from this chapter to strengthen her faith this week?

4

The Gracious Friend

We love because he first loved us.

1 JOHN 4:19

I (CHERYL) LOVE A good cup of tea. I've yet to acquire a taste for coffee, unless it's been doctored with lots of cream and sugar. But tea—well, that's my thing. I also have a collection of teacups: one from a trip to England, another a wedding gift from my brides-maids, a few passed down from my grandmother, and others from here and there. I'm not so sentimental that I simply display my teacups, never to be used. I take a functional approach: use what I have, even if it has special meaning. If a cup breaks, chips, or loses its saucer, I figure that's part of its story.

Recently I've been meeting with two younger women, encourag-ing them through difficult seasons in their marriages. It's amazing to see how the Lord has been growing and sustaining them as they're learning to be godly wives. In one conversation, I told my two friends that they're like teacups being filled, not just to the brim but to overflowing. It's as if tea is spilling everywhere, out of the cup, into the saucer, and onto the table. The Lord is pouring his lovingkindness into their lives, and as he does, love is spilling over into the lives of their husbands. It reminds me of what King David said: "My cup overflows. Surely goodness and mercy shall follow me all the days of my life" (Ps. 23:5–6).

"We love because he first loved us" (1 John 4:19). My friends' marriages are an example of this, but it's also true of all our relationships as believers, beginning with our relationship to God. We love *him* because he first loved us. We were once dead in sin, unable to respond to his love, "but God, being rich in mercy, because of the great love with which he loved us, even when we were dead in our trespasses, made us alive together with Christ" (Eph. 2:4–5). God's love enlivens us to love him.

We also love *one another* because he first loved us. Jesus said, "A new commandment I give to you, that you love one another: just as I have loved you, you also are to love one another. By this all people will know that you are my disciples, if you have love for one another" (John 13:34–35). A mark, or an outflow, of a disciple of Christ is love for other believers. Having uniquely experienced his grace, we learn from his love and extend it to others. We show love because we've been loved. We give grace because we've received grace.

Jesus is our perfect gracious friend. When teaching his disciples how to love one another, he explained, "Greater love has no one than this, that someone lay down his life for his friends" (John 15:13). A few short hours later Jesus fulfilled those very words. On the cross, he showed us that the essence of love is sacrifice—the laying down of one's life for the good of another, from the smallest gesture of kindness to the greatest act of service. Jesus loved us to the point of death even though we didn't deserve such love. But he loved us anyway, and that is grace.

A Gracious Friend

My sister, Susan, has been a gracious friend to me (Caroline) for as long as I can remember. Whether we've lived in the same house as children or on opposite sides of the world as adults, Susan has been a constant and positive presence in my life. I've learned not to take her friendship for granted, especially as I've seen many other sister relationships fade over the years. I know she'll always love me, not simply because she's my sister, but because she knows how to love well.

Susan is good at initiating meaningful conversations. She not only asks surface questions but also questions that reveal my heart. She listens well and is unafraid to speak truth to me when I need to hear it. It may be suggestions for decluttering my house, advice for how to love my children, or insights she's gleaned from her daily devotions. Susan always has something to say that's good for me: a little encouragement, a gentle reproof, or some needed wisdom.

Susan is also a friend who willingly makes sacrifices. Because we now live in different parts of the country, and she knows I'm not much of a planner, Susan makes special arrangements for us to see each other, often sacrificing her time and resources to make it happen. I'll always cherish one relaxing getaway when we shopped, browsed art galleries, and laughed into the evening. On another trip during a hard time in my life, Susan provided a sympathetic shoulder to cry on and the kind of loving encouragement that only a close friend can give.

The qualities I admire in Susan I also see in our Lord. Although she isn't perfect, Susan displays the fruit of the Spirit, especially love, kindness, and goodness, and she encourages the same in me. The older I get, the more I appreciate how her cup of grace overflows into my life. When I need a friend, she's available. When I need wise counsel, she gives it. When I lack, she prays and sacrifices. Susan loves like Jesus loves.

The Character of a Gracious Friend

In chapter 3 we discussed how God's grace teaches us to speak with grace. In this chapter we want to help you further explore how to imitate Christ in your character, conversation, and conduct as you share God's truth with others. How can your life—your cup—overflow with grace? How can you live so that your message is heard? How can you help, and not hinder, others' reception of God's word? To sum it up, how can you be a gracious friend like Jesus?

Let's begin by considering the character of a gracious friend, the qualities that describe her inner person. Who she is on the *inside* defines her as a friend more than her personality, appearance, and shared interests. The gracious friend is adorned with what Peter calls "the hidden person of the heart," which attracts others and pleases God (1 Pet. 3:4). Three core qualities mark a gracious woman whose life serves as an effective platform for sharing God's word with others. She is Spirit-filled, humble, and loyal.

1. A Gracious Friend Is Spirit-Filled

Being filled with the Spirit is essential if we are to imitate Jesus in our relationships. When God saved us, we were washed and renewed by the Spirit (Titus 3:5), baptized into the body of Christ by the Spirit (1 Cor. 12:13), and indwelt by the Spirit (Rom. 8:9–11). Yet God still commands us to "be filled with the Spirit" (Eph. 5:18). What exactly does that mean? To be Spirit-filled means to be Spirit-controlled—to live under the control, or influence, of the Spirit of God. Those who are filled with the Spirit "live continually under the influence of the Spirit by letting the Word control them. . . . Being filled with the Spirit is living in the conscious presence of the Lord Jesus Christ, letting his mind, through the Word, dominate everything that is thought and done."[1]

The gracious friend, then, delights in the word of God and continually yields herself to the Spirit of God by forsaking sin and pursuing godliness (Rom. 8:13). As she fills her mind with Scripture, the Spirit's influence increases in her life. Saturated with the word, the fruit of the Spirit flourishes in her life and provides spiritual nourishment for all who are near. They are drawn to her because of her thriving and fruitful relationship with God.

Do you desire to be a gracious friend? Then be filled with the Spirit: "*Let the word of Christ dwell in you richly*, teaching and admonishing one another in all wisdom, singing psalms and hymns and spiritual songs, with thankfulness in your hearts to God" (Col. 3:16).

2. A Gracious Friend Is Humble

Imagine two different conversations with two friends you haven't seen for a while. In the first conversation, your friend shares what's happening in her life, but she's also happily interested in yours. She asks how you're doing and listens intently because she sincerely cares about you. In the second conversation, your other friend doesn't stop talking about herself. She's focused on her own interests and seems indifferent to you and your life. If she happens to ask about you, somehow the topic of conversation quickly returns to her.

Which of these two friends exhibits humility? The first, of course. She defers to you, selflessly giving you the opportunity to share about yourself. The other friend is self-centered. Her conversation shows that her heart is consumed with her own wants, needs, and opinions. With a humble heart, the gracious friend doesn't think highly of herself; rather, she gives preference to others with kindness, even with her words. She's learned to not be selfish or conceited, but to consider others more important than herself (Phil. 2:3).

Humility doesn't come easy. We're all naturally bent toward pride. It's often revealed in our sinful attitudes, from arrogance to selfishness to self-pity. Given its strong pull in our lives, you may wonder, "How can I overcome pride and grow in humility?" To develop a humble heart, learn from Christ and follow his example:

> Have this mind among yourselves, which is yours in Christ Jesus, who, though he was in the form of God, did not count equality with God a thing to be grasped, but emptied himself, by taking the form of a servant, being born in the likeness of men. And being found in human form, he humbled himself by becoming obedient to the point of death, even death on a cross. (Phil. 2:5–8)

Jesus, the eternal Son of God, laid aside his exaltation with the Father in heaven to become a man—impoverished, despised, and rejected. The King of glory humbled himself as an obedient servant unto death for your sake. Because of his sacrifice, you're blessed with every spiritual blessing (Eph. 1:3). Make Christlike humility your aim: "Let each of you look not only to his own interests, but also to the interests of others" (Phil. 2:4). Don't seek to be exalted; rather, have the mindset of Christ that desires to honor and bless others. Be thoughtful about how to love well, even at your own expense.[2]

In addition, to be a humble friend you must admit your own sinfulness. If you're honest with the Lord and yourself about your own struggles and shortcomings, then you won't be shocked, judgmental, or easily offended when a friend shares her sin and failures with you. To respond with humility, own the fact that you're a sinner as well (Rom. 3:23). You both need the same Savior.

3. A Gracious Friend Is Loyal

In our own times of trouble, these two promises have often comforted us: "I will never leave you nor forsake you" (Heb. 13:5), and "If we are faithless, he remains faithful—for he cannot deny himself" (2 Tim. 2:13). In the first, we're reminded that Christ will never abandon us. In the second, we're reassured that when we're weak in faith or obedience, he's still trustworthy to keep his promises. What can separate us from his love? Absolutely nothing. That's true loyalty.

A gracious friend is loyal like Jesus. Her loyalty "implies a faithfulness that is steadfast in the face of any temptation to renounce, desert, or betray."[3] Her love for others and her commitment to their good is unwavering. You can always count on her. Like a priceless gemstone, her friendship is precious and rare: "Many claim to have unfailing love, but a faithful person who can find?" (Prov. 20:6 NIV).

Consider your loyalty as a friend. Are you loyal regardless of your loved one's circumstances? Do you rejoice when she rejoices and weep when she weeps (Rom. 12:15)? When a friend is blessed in a special way, be happy and thankful instead of indifferent or jealous. Acknowledge and celebrate the victories in her life. Share her joy! But when your loved one experiences trials or failures, don't leave her side. Recognize her difficulties and heartaches—

such as a financial setback, a sick or rebellious child, or a death in the family—and support her however you can. Let her know you sympathize with her and are praying for her. Consider how you can practically help to relieve her suffering, even in small ways.

Also ask yourself: "Am I loyal even when my friend doesn't deserve it or the friendship becomes too hard? Am I a friend who bears, believes, hopes, and endures all things with her (1 Cor. 13:7)?" Maybe your friend has mistreated you, is entangled in sin, or struggles with long-term depression or anxiety. As a Christian sister seeking to love like Christ, keep pursuing her. Continue reaching out to her, encouraging her in the right direction, and bearing patiently with her shortcomings. Address her spiritual needs when it's appropriate and persist in your friendship. "Love never ends" (1 Cor. 13:8).

The Conversation of a Gracious Friend

A gracious friend is not only known by her character but also by her words. King Solomon wisely observed, "Oil and perfume make the heart glad, so a man's counsel is sweet to his friend" (Prov. 27:9 NASB). Just like oil and perfume can rejuvenate a troubled body or heart, the conversation of a gracious friend brings comfort, healing, and strength. She's learned from personal experience and by much practice that "the most pleasant conversation . . . promotes the prosperity of the soul."[4] The words of a gracious friend are self-controlled, wise, and hopeful, and those who hear her speak are the better for it.

1. A Gracious Friend Speaks with Self-Control

Have you ever heard a child banging on a piano, making up her own music? It's cute for a few minutes, and then it can become annoying. But give that child piano lessons, and within a few years you'll enjoy hearing her play. Careful instruction and self-discipline will have provided her with skillful control of the instrument so that when she does play the piano, others truly enjoy it.

Self-control means "restraint exercised over one's own impulses, emotions, or desires."[5] Just as an accomplished pianist has learned proper technique to beautifully express herself at the piano, a gracious friend has learned self-control so that she can carefully express herself with words that bless others. But the woman lacking restraint in her speech is harmful to everyone. Proverbs 25:28 warns that someone "without self-control is like a city broken into and left without walls." Unless self-control guards the mouth, foolish and sinful speech easily tumbles out.

How can you gain self-control over your speech? First, check your heart, for your speech originates *within* you (Luke 6:45). Self-controlled speech begins with submitting control of your heart to the Lord. Confess and turn from ungodly thoughts, motives, and attitudes in your heart, and your words will begin to reflect the Christlike changes in your inner person.

Second, think before you speak. It's tempting to speak your mind and even congratulate yourself for being a straight shooter, but that attitude leads to ruin. Instead, thoughtfully guard your words (Prov. 13:3). Ask yourself: "Is what I'm about to say true, kind, and necessary?"[6] To be true, your words must be free from falsehood and exaggeration. To be kind, your words must be considerate and gentle. To be necessary, your words must be needful in the moment to accomplish what is good and right.

Third, speak with self-control by using your words to promote unity, and never division: Be "eager to maintain the unity of the Spirit in the bond of peace" (Eph. 4:3). Seek and grant forgiveness, speak highly of others, and learn to resolve conflict biblically.[7] Guard against gossip by keeping others' confidences to yourself, not spreading rumors, and refusing to entertain damaging information. Protect the reputations of others, for a gracious friend is not slanderous but trustworthy with her words (Prov. 11:13).

2. A Gracious Friend Speaks with Wisdom

Wise words are characterized by "deep understanding, keen discernment, and . . . sound judgment."[8] They communicate the application of knowledge to real-life situations. It's like my (Cheryl's) friend, Sheila, who recently gave my daughter and me sewing lessons. We could have tried to learn by ourselves how to sew, but Sheila is a skilled seamstress who was able to help us avoid beginner mistakes and master the basics. Similarly, the wise words of a gracious friend teach us how to live skillfully for God's glory. She shows us how to put God's word into practice. She "opens her mouth with wisdom, and the teaching of kindness is on her tongue" (Prov. 31:26).

To be a woman of wisdom, begin by fearing the Lord (Prov. 1:7). The fear of the Lord is

> that *indefinable mixture of reverence and pleasure, joy and awe* which fills our hearts when we realize who God is and what he has done for us. It is *a love for God* which is so great that we would be ashamed to do anything that would displease or grieve him, and makes us happiest when we are doing what pleases him.[9]

To understand who God is and what he's done for you, look at his creation and be in awe of his power and majesty. Gaze upon his grace in the gospel and marvel at his justice and mercy. If you revere and love the Lord supremely, the joy of your life will be to avoid what displeases him and pursue that which honors him.

Next, study the Scriptures: "For the LORD gives wisdom; from his mouth come knowledge and understanding" (Prov. 2:6). Like Ezra, set your heart to know God's word so that you can obey it in your own life and then share it with others (Ezra 7:10). Through diligent and consistent Bible study, conform your thoughts and speech to the source of true wisdom.

In addition, pray for wisdom: "Open my eyes, that I may behold wondrous things out of your law" (Ps. 119:18). Ask the Lord to help you understand and apply the Scriptures to your life. The prayer for wisdom is a prayer that the Lord delights to answer (1 Kings 3:10–12). You can pray with confidence knowing that God will grant you wisdom as you search his word and ask in faith.

3. A Gracious Friend Speaks with Hope

The words of a gracious friend foster hope because they are *full* of hope. Her words are characterized by confidence in the attributes and promises of God. She has a high view of him, and she inspires others to trust him with reminders of his faithfulness. Her hope in the Lord is contagious and brings joy to those around her (Prov. 10:28). For the believer, the word *hope* is not an expression of doubt or uncertainty. Instead, it communicates a secure faith in God. One pastor explained that hope "is not simply a 'wish' (I wish that such-and-such would take place); rather, it is that which latches on to the certainty of the promises of the future that God has made."[10] Hope is a confident expectation of his goodness and faithfulness.

Do your words inspire hope in God? Do you encourage others with God's past faithfulness and future promises? Speak with joyful certainty about his enduring love. We all need reminders that the

Lord will be our help in every circumstance and that he'll always be faithful. Just as Aaron upheld the weary arms of his brother, Moses, throughout battle (Ex. 17:11–13), strengthen and uphold others' faith with Scripture and your personal expressions of hope in God.

Sometimes you may offer hope with a simple comment, and sometimes you may have opportunity to share specific Bible verses to encourage another's hope in God. To be genuine, share verses with your loved one that have *personally* helped you in the past. Briefly explain how a particular scripture has strengthened your own hope in God. For example, Matthew 11:28 has been a comfort to me (Caroline) through many trials. I often share it with others who are under heavy burdens to encourage their faith in Jesus: "Come to me, all who labor and are heavy laden, and I will give you rest."

We have one more thought to share with you about encouraging hope in others: proceed with caution. Keep in mind how your hopeful words could come across as unfeeling or hurtful to a friend who is suffering. Be discerning when offering hope: Are you being sensitive to the timing and content of what you're saying? Are you allowing your loved one to express her concerns and process the biblical truth she already knows? Beware of bombarding her with Christian clichés instead of taking the time to have meaningful conversations about her trials and God's faithfulness. Sometimes it's best to be quiet, and sometimes it's best to simply sprinkle hope in what you say. When in doubt, gently ask your friend if you can share with her the hope that God has given you.

The Conduct of a Gracious Friend

Throughout this chapter we have learned of the gracious friend's character and conversation. Let's now consider the gracious friend's conduct—what she does. The old saying, "The proof is in the pudding," means you can judge the quality of something once you experience it. That's especially true of friendship. What a friend *does* reveals the kind of friend she *is*.

If you want your words to be well received, check to see that your conduct paves the way for God's word to be shared instead of its throwing up a roadblock. James, the half-brother of Jesus, made this point: "Who is wise and understanding among you? By his good conduct let him show his works in the meekness of wisdom" (James 3:13). Think about your behavior as a friend: Do you listen carefully? Do you forgive readily? Do you serve sacrificially?

1. A Gracious Friend Listens

In *Anne of Green Gables*, Anne is adopted by two elderly siblings, Marilla and Matthew Cuthbert. They lovingly welcome Anne into their home, but she still longs for a close friend. Anne asks Marilla, "Do you think that I shall ever have a bosom friend in Avonlea? . . . A bosom friend—an intimate friend, you know—a really kindred spirit to whom I can confide my innermost soul. I've dreamed of meeting her all my life."[11] Anne, like most of us, desired a trustworthy friend who would truly listen to her heart.

A gracious friend warmly welcomes you into her life and gently steps into yours. One of the most significant ways she does this is by listening intently. She seeks to truly know you, doesn't interrupt or get distracted, and never makes you feel rushed or foolish. She's genuinely interested in hearing you, and when you spend time with her, you know you're loved.

If there's one thing we want to encourage you about listening well, it's this: listen to gain understanding. You can't give appropriate truth to a loved one without first knowing what she's really going through. The encouragement and advice you give needs to match her concerns, and that requires your patience. Take time to listen instead of making assumptions or quickly offering solutions (Prov. 18:13). Gently ask questions that clarify the situation and reveal her heart. Proverbs 20:5 says, "The purpose in a man's heart is like deep water, but a man of understanding will draw it out." Like lowering a pail into a deep well, a gracious friend asks questions to draw out another's thoughts and feelings. Let *her* talk, and you'll be better prepared to respond with wisdom and grace.

2. A Gracious Friend Forgives

Have you ever left a conversation thinking you might have said something that could be misinterpreted? You keep replaying a foolish remark, an awkward attempt at humor, or some friendly teasing that now seems insensitive. Or if you're anything like us, maybe you've hurt someone with a sinful attitude or response. Afterward, you feel convicted and genuinely sorry. You confess your sin to the Lord, but you know you must go make things right with the other person. And yet you wonder, "Will she forgive me?"

Every day we encounter opportunities for misunderstanding and offense. Those around us can't help but be affected by all the prickly edges of our personality, words, and actions, and we can't help but be affected by theirs also. But a gracious friend has learned how to overlook offenses (Prov. 19:11). She's more committed to extending grace than holding a grudge. How is she able to do what is so unnatural?

The gracious friend understands she's a recipient of grace. She knows that she's been forgiven much, and so she loves much and readily forgives those who have sinned against her (Eph. 4:32). Peter once struggled with understanding forgiveness and asked Jesus, "Lord, how often will my brother sin against me, and I forgive him?" (Matt. 18:21). Jesus then told a parable about an unforgiving servant to show us the importance of forgiving one another as God has forgiven our *enormous* sin debt against him. We must forgive as we've been forgiven. In the parable, the servant's master made that point when he asked, "Should not you have had mercy on your fellow servant, as I had mercy on you?" (Matt. 18:33).

Years later Peter wrote, "Above all, keep loving one another earnestly, since love covers a multitude of sins" (1 Pet. 4:8). Peter had learned forgiveness firsthand from his closest friend, Jesus. After Peter denied knowing him three times, Jesus forgave Peter and restored their relationship (John 18:15–27; 21:15–23). As you think about your closest friend, you'll probably realize that she has a forgiving spirit, just like the Lord. She doesn't hold grudges against you; rather, she forgives you when you've been insensitive or unkind. You could never maintain a relationship with her without forgiveness.

So how can you be a friend who forgives readily? If someone mistreats you in a small or insignificant way, willingly overlook the offense and cover it with love. If the sin against you is more significant and you don't seem able to overlook it, talk through the issues with the other person and seek to be reconciled. Whether the offender seeks your forgiveness or not, have an attitude of forgiveness toward her. Don't dwell on the offense, don't hold it against her, and certainly don't gossip about it. As far as it depends on you, live at peace with her, treating her with grace as the Lord has treated you (Rom. 12:18).[12]

3. A Gracious Friend Serves

Think back to someone who has served you in the past. What need was met, and how? Once on a long road trip, my (Cheryl's) family had car trouble, and a family we'd never met before provided us with dinner and a place to spend the night. I also remember how my cousin used her vacation time to fly across the country and help me care for my premature twins. I recall my mother dropping everything to talk with me on the phone for as long as I needed her—more times than I can count. Every act of kindness has communicated love.

One of the reasons God redeemed you is so that you would serve others. Paul wrote, "You were called to freedom, brothers. Only do not use your freedom as an opportunity for the flesh, but through love serve one another. For the whole law is fulfilled in one word: 'You shall love your neighbor as yourself'" (Gal. 5:13–14). The command to love your neighbor is so important that it's called the "royal law," being only second in line to loving the King himself (James 2:8). We love others when we meet their spiritual and physical needs with the same commitment we have to meeting our own, and with the same fervency with which we love the Lord.

How can you be a faithful friend who serves? Remember how Christ served you, and you'll be motivated to serve like him. Mark 10:45 says, "The Son of Man came not to be served but to serve, and to give his life as a ransom for many." From this verse, you can draw two important lessons about serving like Christ. First, serve *intentionally*. Jesus anticipated your needs, purposed to meet them, and then did it: he came to serve. Look beyond your own needs and take initiative to know the needs of others. Consider how you can be a blessing to someone else, and then get busy. When it comes to serving others, it's not the thought that counts; it's the actual doing.

Second, serve *sacrificially*. Jesus served to the point of the ultimate sacrifice—he gave his life. When you serve in a way that requires you to give up something for another, you reflect the love of Christ. Don't hold tightly to your time, money, energy, and belongings. Joyfully do good and share with others, "for such sacrifices are pleasing to God" (Heb. 13:16). Remember that when you sacrificially serve those who can't repay you, you're serving the Lord (see Matt. 25:31–40).

Are you a gracious friend who intentionally and sacrificially serves? If you realize you need to grow in this area of your life, follow Christ's example and begin serving where you see a need. Or maybe you've been serving others faithfully, but you feel discouraged because you haven't received the same kind of care or appreciation in return. Regardless of your situation, in faith and obedience pursue being a servant, and entrust yourself to your Lord as you do good (1 Pet. 4:19). Serve God by serving others and trust him for opportunities to speak his truth with grace as you do so. Persevere in loving others as you've been loved by Christ, your perfect and gracious friend.

REFLECTION QUESTIONS

1. Do you have a gracious friend who displays Christlike love toward you? List some ways she's loved you well. What qualities do you appreciate in her?

2. Love should "spill" from your life into the lives of others. Read John 13:34–35 and 1 John 4:15–21. In these verses, who is the source of that love? How is the believer's relationship to Jesus described, and how does it impact others?

3. What three qualities of a gracious friend's character are highlighted in this chapter? Describe them in your own words and with key

Scripture verses. Which quality do you need to develop in your own life?

4. What three qualities of a gracious friend's conversation are high-lighted in this chapter? Describe them in your own words and with key Scripture verses. Which quality do you need to develop in your own life?

5. What three aspects of a gracious friend's conduct are highlighted in this chapter? Describe them in your own words and with key Scripture verses. Which quality do you need to develop in your own life?

6. Read Philippians 2:1–11. In what ways has Christ been gracious to you? How does his example motivate you to be a gracious friend?

5

When Grace Is Tested

Better is open rebuke than hidden love. . . .
Faithful are the wounds of a friend.

PROVERBS 27:5–6

HAVE YOU EVER TRIED to give medicine to a child who didn't want to take it? If you haven't, you can probably imagine the difficulty for a mother whose sick daughter needs to take medication and yet stubbornly refuses. With tight lips, clenched teeth, and maybe even some tears, the little girl has no intention of opening her mouth. The mother's patience is put to the test as she coaxes, pleads, and bargains with the child. Her daughter, however, still won't cooperate. She doesn't understand how much her mother loves her and wants what's best for her little girl.

Like a devoted mother giving medicine to a sick child, maybe you're trying to help a loved one spiritually. You're offering her encouragement or instruction from God's word, but she's not receiving it well. You're trying to speak truth with grace, yet the truth is being resisted, and your grace toward her is being tested. You may desire to share Scripture with her, but you didn't realize it could be so hard to love someone in this way. Perhaps you're wondering, "How should I respond to someone if she doesn't readily receive what God's word has to say? What if she's indifferent to what I share with her from Scripture or becomes upset with me? Should I continue trying to talk with her about her problem? What would God have me to do?"

We also have asked these kinds of questions and have found that Scripture provides abundant wisdom for knowing how to respond to those who resist God's word or mistreat us for bringing it to bear on their lives. In this chapter we'll look at five types of believers who have difficulty receiving and applying God's truth and how we should respond biblically and lovingly to each of them.

The Wound of a Faithful Friend

I (Caroline) will be the first to admit that it's hard to hear someone point out a weakness or sin in my life, even when she speaks graciously and truthfully. I'm reminded of the time when my friend Ana sat me down and addressed a concern she had about me. It wasn't easy to receive what she said, but because I valued our friendship, I listened.

I've been a quiet and shy person all my life. As a child, you probably wouldn't have noticed me in a classroom full of students. As a teen, I didn't want any attention drawn to me, so I avoided sharing my thoughts and interests with others. Even today, my favorite hobbies are those done alone: stamp collecting, reading, and needlework. Some might call me an introvert.

In her gentle way, Ana explained to me that women in our church didn't feel that they knew me, even though I was the pastor's wife. My shy nature was hindering my relationships because I wasn't offering the two-way communication needed to love other believers or to be loved by them. Ana's words caused me to think carefully about why I held myself back, not letting other women into my life. Was I fearful and self-protective? Was I too lazy to reach out? Was I simply self-absorbed? As uncomfortable as it was, I was forced to consider the motives for my aloofness. I learned there was a selfishness in my heart that had to be replaced with love. I realized that just as Christ didn't live to please himself, neither was I to live to please myself (Rom. 15:3).

Ana's exhortation stung, even though she spoke with kindness and compassion. My first thought was, "I'm so embarrassed that Ana sees a weakness in me." But the more I thought about what Ana said, the more I realized that she loved me, had my best interests in mind, and wanted to help expand my ministry to others. She taught me that in my personal weakness, God's grace is sufficient, and his power is perfected in me (2 Cor. 12:9). I'm sure that Ana, not knowing exactly how I'd respond, originally debated within herself whether to say anything to me at all. I'm so glad she did.

Ana continued to encourage me to build relationships with women in our church and community. I admit that change hasn't come quickly. Today I'm still more comfortable speaking one-on-one than in group conversations, where I prefer to listen on the sidelines. But I've matured in my willingness and ability to make friends, to reach out to those in need, and even to teach God's word to large groups of women—thanks to a godly friend who was loving enough to tell me the truth and patient enough to help me grow.

Withdrawn Wendy

As we consider how to respond to believers who are having a hard time receiving and applying God's word, let's begin by looking at

Withdrawn Wendy. Wendy's been through a lot. Maybe she's been deeply hurt, and she's overwhelmed with picking up the pieces of her life. Maybe she's ashamed of what someone has done to her or what she's done to someone else, and she finds it difficult to talk about. Wendy may believe it's easier to ignore her problems or face them alone. She might think there's nothing you can do to help her, or that you might not be able to understand her or her circumstances.

Out of loving concern for Wendy, you've tried to talk with her and to give godly encouragement. But at best, Wendy keeps her conversations with you short and shallow, and at worst she avoids you altogether. You know it's not good for Wendy to pull away from those who truly love her, yet you feel at a loss to know what to do. How can you care for Wendy if she doesn't seem to want your help?

First, don't make assumptions about Wendy. Just because she's not talking with you doesn't mean she's not working through her problems or that she's straying from the Lord. In 1 Samuel 1, Eli the priest assumed Hannah was drunk, but instead she was earnestly and quietly praying for a child. When Eli questioned her about her unusual behavior, she replied, "I am a woman troubled in spirit. . . . I have been pouring out my soul before the LORD" (1 Sam. 1:15). Don't judge Wendy in her silence. Instead, pray for her until she's ready to talk with you.

Second, when you do have an opportunity to speak with Wendy, be patient and gentle. Understand she has reasons for being withdrawn, and it may take time for her to open up to you. Remember that a gracious friend will listen carefully and seek to understand (Prov. 20:5). When it's appropriate, ask open-ended questions, and don't force or rush her answers. Reassure Wendy that you won't be shocked by what she shares because you know that everyone has real problems and heartaches. Be sensitive to discern when she's reached her limit in the conversation, and then be willing to let it go until another time.

Third, if Wendy chooses not to talk with you about whatever is troubling her, you can still remind her of God's promise that if she humbles herself before the Lord, he will draw near to her (James 4:8). God is Wendy's ultimate helper. Encourage her to continually seek him so that she will find the mercy and grace she needs (Heb. 4:16). Remind Wendy of God's lovingkindness toward her: his saving grace through Christ, his Spirit that lives within her, his comfort in the word and prayer, and the gift of other believers with whom to fellowship and worship (Heb. 10:25). Continue to pray for Wendy. Ask God to provide her with the spiritual encouragement and guidance that only he can give, and ask him to provide you with wisdom to know when and how to approach her again.

Angry Angela
On the other hand, you might be trying to speak truth to Angry Angela. Angela is often angry about all kinds of things and at all sorts of people, such as family and friends, people at work and church, strangers at the store and in traffic, and others on the Internet and TV. Since you're one of the people closest to Angela, she often unloads her anger on you. And because you care about her—and maybe even feel sorry for her—you put up with Angela's complaining, harsh words, and bitterness. But you find that being around her is so discouraging!

"A man of wrath stirs up strife, and one given to anger causes much transgression" (Prov. 29:22). Like angry Cain, who murdered Abel, and like jealous Saul, who continually persecuted David, Angela has allowed her anger to drive her to make numerous sinful choices accompanied by bad consequences. When you try to provide her with wisdom and perspective, she verbally attacks you, often dismissing you as simplistic, misunderstanding, or even cruel and uncaring.

In time, Angela needs to address her anger problem, and there are various biblical resources you can share with Angela to help her with that.[1] But right now, our intention is to help you know how to respond to Angela in a godly way when she becomes angry at you for offering biblical advice or admonition. First, be slow to speak (James 1:19). Take a moment to choose your words carefully so that you speak with wisdom and self-control. Second, defuse the conflict. Respond with a soft answer (Prov. 15:1), and be prepared to excuse yourself from the conversation until a later time when she may be ready to listen (Prov. 17:14).

Third, bless in return. If Angela lashes out at you, don't respond in a like manner. Overlook the offense with an attitude of forgiveness (Prov. 19:11), pray for her (Matt. 5:44), and find ways to be kind to Angela even though she's mistreated you (Rom. 12:21).

Lastly, be careful not to be influenced by Angela's anger and become angry like her. Anger can be contagious (Prov. 22:24–25), so stay close enough to Angela to lovingly speak truth into her life, but not so close that anger takes root in your own life as well.

Defensive Delaney

Have you met Defensive Delaney? You may already know her without realizing it. Unless you offer her advice, disagree with her, or provide a different perspective, you probably won't have any conflict with Delaney. But the moment she senses you have an opposing opinion or recognize a flaw in her, her defenses go up. Delaney becomes self-justifying and self-protecting, explaining her thoughts and actions so that you'll approve, even though she often says she doesn't care what other people think. *Nothing* is Delaney's fault—other people and her circumstances get the blame.

Proverbs 28:13 provides both warning and hope for Delaney: "Whoever conceals his transgressions will not prosper, but he who confesses and forsakes them will obtain mercy." If Delaney continually denies personal responsibility when she's given biblical advice and correction, she'll suffer more hardship as her heart becomes increasingly hardened to the truth. Her relationships will become difficult, if not almost impossible, to maintain. Yet God provides a way for Delaney to overcome her defensiveness and its consequences. If she'll admit when she's wrong and confess her sin, God will forgive and teach her to live humbly and honestly with herself and others (1 John 1:8–9).

So, how can you help Defensive Delaney when speaking truth into her life? Before saying anything, make a personal commitment to avoid quarreling with her. Pray that she'll be receptive and that you'll remain calm. Instead of speaking in generalities that could easily be dismissed, be very specific when pointing out a sin in her life that needs to be addressed. To help Delaney understand that you're not simply giving her your own opinion, it's important that you provide her with appropriate Scripture passages that support your concerns (1 Thess. 2:13; 2 Tim. 3:16).

To be fair, you can acknowledge to Delaney the presence of difficult people and circumstances in her life; however, you should also explain that she's still responsible before God to respond to them in biblical, godly ways. She needs to learn that she can't blame anyone else for her own attitudes and behaviors, because they reflect the desires and motives that are in her *own* heart (Luke 6:45). Finally, don't remain silent because you fear Delaney's defensive responses. You are genuinely loving her when you speak truth into her life (Prov. 27:5–6). Be faithful and courageous in the Lord to say what must be said, and then entrust the outcome to him.

Struggling Stacy

We're sure you know Struggling Stacy. You see her at work, school, church, or even at home. You probably sometimes see her in the mirror too. Stacy struggles with a besetting sin. It plagues her, and she often falls into it easily, even though she's grieved by it. It may be discontentment, jealousy, lust, impatience, anger, fear, or gluttony—the list could go on. Whatever the sin is and however it manifests in her life, she knows it's wrong and wants to overcome it. Stacy loves the Lord and desires to obey him, but she feels stuck in an endless cycle of falling into the same sin. Some days she's victorious; other days she gives in to the sin and is weighed down with guilt and discouragement.

Stacy is a lot like the apostle Peter. Proverbs 24:16 describes their common struggle: "The righteous falls seven times and rises again." Peter repeatedly battled unbelief during the three years he spent with Jesus. One moment Peter's faith was strong, but the next moment it was weak. He stepped out of a boat and walked on water, but when he took his eyes off Jesus, he sank (Matt. 14:29–30). He declared Jesus to be the Christ, the Son of the living God, but then he scolded Jesus for saying he must suffer (Matt. 16:16, 21–22). He promised never to deny Jesus, but later that night he lied, saying he didn't even know Jesus (Matt. 26:35, 69–72). But unlike his fellow disciple Judas Iscariot, who ended his life in despair over his sin, Peter kept looking to Jesus. Peter stayed in the struggle, and the Lord was merciful to him.

God can use you as an instrument of his mercy in Stacy's life. She's fighting against sin, and she needs your loving support as she learns to live in obedience to Christ. First, remind Stacy of God's promises of forgiveness and faithfulness in the gospel. In Christ, she's no longer a slave to sin or under condemnation, and nothing can separate her from the love of God (Rom. 6:22; 8:1, 38–39). Second, continue to encourage her with relevant truth from God's word (Heb. 3:13). If she's ignorant of biblical truth, faithfully and gently teach her. If she doesn't know how to apply the Scriptures to her situation, help her with practical suggestions.

Third, provide Stacy with intentional, personal accountability. On a regular basis, ask her specific questions about her struggles and pray with her about them. When you pray, encourage Stacy to confess her failures, to give thanks for the victories, and to ask for strength to obey. Continually direct her to the Lord in his word. Read it together and discuss how it applies to her life. As you walk alongside Stacy, don't grow weary and give up on her; rather, continually encourage and build her up in Christ (1 Thess. 5:11).

Rebellious Rita

Lastly, we come to Rebellious Rita. Unlike Struggling Stacy, Rebellious Rita is no longer fighting against sin. She now embraces it. Although Rita has professed faith in the past, her current sinful choices reveal that she's rejecting the authority of Christ and his word in her life. Despite the consequences for herself, she's willfully pursuing sin over obedience and worldliness over godliness. Rita isn't interested in hearing biblical truth from you; instead, she's intent on going her own way.

Two key passages explain how you should respond to Rebellious Rita. The first is Galatians 6:1: "Brothers, if anyone is caught in any transgression, you who are spiritual should restore him in a spirit of gentleness. Keep watch on yourself, lest you too be tempted." We learn important lessons from this passage. First, don't ignore Rita or her choices. God expects you, as one who's walking in obedience to the Spirit, to address the sin in Rita's life. The purpose isn't to punish or condemn her but to draw her back from her sin and to help restore her to a right relationship with God and others. Also, speak to Rita with genuine gentleness and humility. Beware of needlessly discrediting your message by approaching her with harshness or arrogance. And, lastly, beware of becoming entangled in Rita's sin or responding to her with a sinful attitude or behavior of your own. As you pray for her repentance, also pray for yourself that you will remain strong in the Lord and not fall into similar temptations.

The second key passage that teaches us how to respond rightly to Rita is Matthew 18:15–17:

> If your brother sins against you, go and tell him his fault, between you and him alone. If he listens to you, you have gained your brother. But if he does not listen, take one or two others along with you, that every charge may be established by the evidence of two or three witnesses. If he refuses to listen to them, tell it to the church. And if he refuses to listen even to the church, let him be to you as a Gentile and a tax collector.

It's significant that Jesus gave these instructions immediately after telling the parable of the lost sheep. The good shepherd loved the lone, straying sheep so much that he left his entire flock to search for it, and he greatly rejoiced when it was found. Seek after Rebellious Rita with this same kind of compassion and concern. Speak with her alone about her sin and call her to repentance. If she doesn't turn from her sin, then take one or two other mature Christians with you to speak with her and call her again to forsake it. If she still doesn't respond, then explain the situation to her church leadership and ask them to join you as you speak with her. If Rita still refuses to repent, it's the responsibility of her church to patiently pursue her and eventually remove her from their fellowship if necessary.[2]

This process of confronting Rita's sin is an act of love toward her. It gives Rita an opportunity to receive godly counsel and exhortation, to repent of the sin in her life, and to be restored to the Lord. If she has no intention of forsaking her sin and living in fellowship with God and his people, then her removal from the church is simply an honest representation of her spiritual condition. At that point, you can love her as you do an unbeliever, but not with the pretense that she belongs to Christ. Continue to pray for the Holy Spirit to convict Rita of her sin and to give her understanding of what is good and right in the sight of God (John 16:8–11).

Times will come when the grace you extend to others is tested, and you might suffer mistreatment or heartache for speaking truth to them in love. When that happens, don't give up. Persevere in your commitment to the Lord and in doing what's good for others, according to his word. Continue to serve Christ by loving his people with truth and grace: "Be steadfast, immovable, always abounding in the work of the Lord, knowing that in the Lord your labor is not in vain" (1 Cor. 15:58).

REFLECTION QUESTIONS

---

1. Read Psalm 141:5. When has another Christian spoken truth into your life such that you found it was difficult to hear at first, but

later you realized it was for your good? What lessons did God teach you through that experience?

2. This chapter highlights how we should biblically respond to those who are withdrawn, angry, defensive, struggling, and rebellious. List the biblical ways to approach each of them as explained in this chapter, along with supporting Scripture verses.

3. Read about how Jesus responded to a Samaritan woman in John 4:1–26, a rich young man in Mark 10:17–22, his enemies in Luke 23:33–37, and Peter in John 21:15–19. What was Jesus's attitude toward each of them? What were his main concerns for each? What does Jesus's example teach you about how to respond when your grace toward others is tested?

4. Read 2 Corinthians 7:8–13 and 1 Thessalonians 2:5–9. How did Paul approach the Corinthians and the Thessalonians in their sin? What did their repentance look like?

5. Do you have a loved one who resembles one of the women in this chapter? What have you learned from this chapter about how to respond to her and to love her well? How will you specifically apply what you've learned to your conversations with her?

6

Truth That Transforms

And we all . . . beholding the glory of the Lord,
are being transformed into the same image
from one degree of glory to another.

2 CORINTHIANS 3:18

WHEN I (CHERYL) WAS in college, I traveled to England on a mission trip with my college choir. We held one of our concerts at Canterbury Cathedral, the center of the worldwide Anglican Church. I don't remember much about our visit to the cathedral, but I do recall being in awe of the cathedral's magnificent architecture and beautiful acoustics. I also remember a comment made by a local missionary who had come to hear us sing. While a few of us visited with him after the concert, the missionary mentioned that Canterbury Cathedral had recently hosted an ecumenical fair. Several world religions were represented at the event, which was held to promote unity and love among those who attended. The missionary commented with great concern, "Love at the expense of truth isn't love."

I've often thought about what the missionary said that day. Love that compromises truth or sacrifices it altogether isn't genuine, biblical love. Truth and love must always go hand in hand, especially as we encourage one another in the Christian life. Think of truth and love as two sides of the same coin: they must always be given together. Paul reminds us of this when he says, "Rather, *speaking the truth in love*, we are to grow up in every way into him who is the head, into Christ" (Eph. 4:15).

In previous chapters, we've discussed how to speak truth *in love*—or as we have explained, *with grace*. Now let's turn our attention to the actual *truth* that we're called to speak. That truth is God's word. Colossians 3:16 commands us to "let the word of Christ dwell in you richly, teaching and admonishing one another in all wisdom." To speak the word into one another's lives with confidence, it's important to have a biblical understanding of the nature of Scripture and what it accomplishes in those who believe. In this chapter we'll look at the essential characteristics of Scripture and the ways it changes us. Our prayer is that you'll be fully assured of the word's transforming power as you speak it with grace.

The Transforming Word

God's word, the whole of the Old and New Testaments, transforms us from the inside out. It changes our thoughts, desires, motives, choices, and behavior—our very lives—when we receive it by faith and respond to it with obedience. As we renew our minds with Scripture, we're transformed to live according to "what is good and acceptable and perfect" in the sight of God (Rom. 12:2). In Psalm 19 King David describes the word's life-changing work in us:

The law of the Lord is perfect,
  reviving the soul;
the testimony of the Lord is sure,
  making wise the simple;
the precepts of the Lord are right,
  rejoicing the heart;
the commandment of the Lord is pure,
  enlightening the eyes;
the fear of the Lord is clean,
  enduring forever;
the rules of the Lord are true,
  and righteous altogether.
More to be desired are they than gold,
  even much fine gold;
sweeter also than honey
  and drippings of the honeycomb.
Moreover, by them is your servant warned;
  in keeping them there is great reward. (vv. 7–11)

Who do you know that needs revival in her soul, wisdom in her circumstances, or joy in her heart? Do you know someone whose spiritual vision has become blurred, who needs to see the Lord and his truth clearly once again? Speak the Scriptures into her life. Give her the priceless gift of God's word; she'll find it more valuable than gold. Feed her the spiritual food that satisfies the soul; she'll find it sweeter than honey. Share God's word with her according to her specific need, and trust the Lord to transform her from within.

The Spirit of God empowers the Scripture's transforming work in us. It's not a change that we can muster ourselves. We need the Spirit to make his word a living reality in us. When God gives us a new heart, he also gives us his Spirit to teach us his truth and to enable us to obey it: "I will give you a new heart. . . . And I will put my Spirit within you, and cause you to walk in my statutes and be careful to obey my rules" (Ezek. 36:26–27). When we look with faith upon the Lord in his word, we are continually being transformed (2 Cor. 3:18). It's the Spirit of God, applying his word to our lives, who makes us more like Jesus. As he empowers us to believe and obey the Scriptures, our lives are changed.

From Shame to Joy

I (Caroline) saw this kind of transformation take place in Gretchen, a young Christian woman who came to me for advice. Through her tears, she shared with me the story of the sexual abuse she had endured at the hands of a religious leader for years. She felt intense shame because those who should have protected her refused to believe her story. Now several years later, Gretchen was willing to discuss what had happened. She wondered if the Bible could help her deal with the recurring nightmares, flashbacks, and questions that intruded into her mind. What would she do if her friends found out about her past? Would she ever be at peace and able to move on with her life? Would Scripture have the answers for her problems?

Gretchen and I began studying the Bible together. She listened carefully as we considered how to interpret her experiences through the lens of Scripture. She clung to passages in the Bible that resonated with her experience, such as the story of Joseph, who was mistreated by his brothers. Gretchen could identify with Joseph. He was misunderstood, blamed, and treated unfairly by many people, yet he was still able to say in the end, "As for you, you meant evil against me, but God meant it for good" (Gen. 50:20). Between our times together, Gretchen read over the verses we had discussed and journaled her thoughts in a notebook. She memorized Bible verses, such as Philippians 4:8–9, to focus her thoughts on truth and not the lies about God and herself that she had believed for so long. Even though we spent a lot of time talking together, it was her time alone with God in his word—reading, studying, and meditating on it—that proved to be the best help of all.

Gretchen began seeing positive changes in her life. Over time her nightmares diminished, and whenever she experienced flashbacks, she read Bible verses that she had posted around her house: on her refrigerator, above her kitchen sink, on her bathroom mirror. As her thinking was renewed, Gretchen learned that God's word is sufficient for her problems. She gained confidence to make new friends, became involved in ministry at her church, and no longer feared condemnation from others. Through the transforming power of the Scriptures, Gretchen could finally address her past and move into her future with joy.

Built on the Rock

Just as the Spirit used the word to transform Gretchen's life, he uses the word to accomplish his good work in *all* who believe. In Matthew 4:4 Jesus said, "Man shall not live by bread alone, but by every word that comes from the mouth of God." With this statement he emphasized the absolute necessity of Scripture in our lives. In the same way that we need to eat nutritious food for our physical well-being, we need to feast on the word of God for our *spiritual* well-being.

Jesus reiterated the supreme role of Scripture in our spiritual growth when he prayed for us: "Sanctify them in the truth; your word is truth" (John 17:17). In the Scriptures, God has revealed all the truth we need for faith and godliness, and yet we're often tempted to turn elsewhere for wisdom and guidance on how to live. We must be careful to not allow worldly wisdom, human opinion, or even our own emotions and intuitions to take precedence over the word of God in our lives. Paul also stresses the importance of solely building our lives on Christ and his truth:

> As you received Christ Jesus the Lord, so walk in him, rooted and built up in him and established in the faith, just as you were taught, abounding in thanksgiving. See to it that no one takes you captive by philosophy and empty deceit, according to human tradition, according to the elemental spirits of the world, and not according to Christ. (Col. 2:6–8)

Consider these questions for a moment: Where did we learn to receive Christ? Where do we learn how to walk in him? How are we rooted, built up, and established in the faith? The only answer is this: in the word of God. Without the word, these things are impossible. Devoid of Scripture, we would be left to our own ignorance and foolishness. We must build our lives on the sure foundation of Christ's word by hearing it, believing it, and ordering our lives according to it. Then we'll be like the wise man who built his house on a rock, instead of the fool who built his house on sand (Matt. 7:24–27). When the rains, winds, and floods of life come upon us, we'll not be shaken because we're firmly established on the word of God.

Four Attributes of the Word

You most likely know that the Bible is a collection of sixty-six books. But did you also know that it was written by forty different authors over a fifteen-hundred-year period, in three different languages and on three different continents? These facts set it apart from any other book the world has ever known, and yet there's more about the Bible that makes it infinitely superior to all other writings. Why should we build our lives on God's word and encourage others to do the same? To answer that question, let's briefly consider these four attributes, or essential characteristics, of Scripture: authority, inerrancy, clarity, and sufficiency.[1]

The Authority of Scripture

We also thank God constantly for this, that when you received the word of God, which you heard from us, you accepted it not as the word of men but as what it really is, the word of God, which is at work in you believers. (1 Thess. 2:13)

The Scriptures are the authority for all that we believe and do because they're the actual words of the living God. All the words in the Bible were inspired by God (or "God-breathed"), and he's providentially preserved his word throughout history for us today (2 Tim. 3:16). Some portions of Scripture record the words that God literally spoke, while other portions record the words that he gave in various ways through men who wrote in their own styles and with their own personalities (Heb. 1:1; 2 Pet. 1:21). In either case, the *ultimate* source of Scripture is God. The Bible reveals who God is and what he requires of us, and for us "to disbelieve or disobey any word of Scripture is to disbelieve or disobey God himself."[2]

The Inerrancy of Scripture

The sum of your word is truth,
and every one of your righteous rules endures forever.
(Ps. 119:160)

The Bible is true in all it says. It is inerrant, meaning it's without error in the original autographs in all that it affirms, whether in history, science, morality, or faith. As we read the Bible, we must take into consideration the authors' ordinary uses of human language (such as generalizations, estimates, metaphors, and the like), but these don't negate Scripture's inerrancy. In other words, "*the Bible always tells the truth*, and . . . it always tells the truth *concerning everything that it talks about.*"[3] In addition, God's word reflects the truthfulness of God himself. He cannot lie, for that would contradict his holy nature (Titus 1:2; Heb. 6:18). Because God is truthful, his word is also truthful: "Every word of God proves true; he is a shield to those who take refuge in him" (Prov. 30:5). Scripture is reliable and trustworthy to direct us in the ways of faith and obedience.

The Clarity of Scripture

> I have more understanding than all my teachers,
>> for your testimonies are my meditation.
> I understand more than the aged,
>> for I keep your precepts. (Ps. 119:99–100)

Another important attribute of Scripture is its clarity. To say that Scripture has clarity means that the average person who reads or hears it can understand its basic message. While it's true that some passages of Scripture may be difficult to interpret, the Bible is generally understandable. It's written in such a way that a child in a Sunday school class and a distinguished professor at a seminary can both read it and comprehend its meaning. This doesn't minimize the importance of sitting under sound preaching or personally and diligently studying the Scriptures, but it does highlight that the

Bible is not a mysterious book that can only be understood by those with special knowledge or training (Acts 17:11; Rom. 10:14). The Scriptures are for all to read, hear, and learn the truth about God, themselves, and the gospel.

The Sufficiency of Scripture

> All Scripture is breathed out by God and profitable for teaching, for reproof, for correction, and for training in righteousness, that the man of God may be complete, equipped for every good work. (2 Tim. 3:16–17)

The Bible contains all the wisdom of God that we need to live in faith and obedience to him. It's fully sufficient for our salvation and sanctification. In 2 Timothy 3:17 we see that God's word prepares, or equips, us for "*every* good work." It's fully capable of making us imitators of Christ in everything—in all we do, think, feel, and believe. All the truth we need to be all that God wants us to be is found in his word: "By it we are *thoroughly furnished for every good work.* . . . Whatever duty we have to do, whatever service is required from us, we may find enough in the Scriptures to furnish us for it."[4]

You might be thinking, "There are lots of things I can think of that the Bible doesn't talk about, so is it true that it's sufficient?" The answer is yes, Scripture is sufficient—meaning that it addresses every issue and circumstance of your life in one way or another so that you can honor God in it. For example, although the Bible doesn't teach you how to change a tire with step-by-step instructions, it *does* teach you how to change a tire—with patience and self-control. Although it doesn't tell you who to marry by name, it *does* tell you who to marry—a man who walks with Christ. The word doesn't explain how to fill out your tax forms line by line, but it *does* tell you how to fill out your tax forms—with honesty and integrity. Are you personally struggling with anxiety, exhaustion, gluttony, or grief? Are you dealing with an angry child, financial problems, or a difficult decision? No matter what you're facing, Scripture is sufficient to provide all you need to glorify God in your circumstances.

The Work of the Word

One afternoon when I (Cheryl) was in high school, I was talking on the phone with a Christian friend and complaining (once again) about some circumstances in my life. I was throwing a first-rate pity party when my friend suddenly said, "Cheryl, I'm going to hang up the phone now. Go read 2 Corinthians 4." I was shocked when she immediately hung up on me, but I went into my bedroom, opened my Bible, and was introduced to a chapter that God would use to teach and change me. Over the next several weeks I devoured 2 Corinthians 4. As I read, studied, and memorized it, my heart was renewed with a Godward joy and purpose. The last three verses of the chapter were especially instructive and encouraging. They reminded me that God was sanctifying me through my trials, and that to endure hardship I had to look beyond my temporary circumstances to the eternal promises that are mine in Christ:

> So we do not lose heart. Though our outer self is wasting away, our inner self is being renewed day by day. For this light momentary affliction is preparing for us an eternal weight of glory beyond all comparison, as we look not to the things that are seen but to the things that are unseen. For the things that are seen are transient, but the things that are unseen are eternal. (2 Cor. 4:16–18)

Can you remember a time in your life when a passage of Scripture made a significant impact on you? Can you identify smaller, less dramatic ways that God's word influences and directs you on a daily basis? The way God used 2 Corinthians 4 in my life is just one of the countless stories of how God uses his word to transform his people. Scripture is at work in all who receive it by faith. When we first receive the gospel as revealed in the word, it saves our souls (James 1:21). But once we are saved, the word has an ongoing effect in us. What is Scripture doing in us? How are we being transformed?

First, Scripture increases our knowledge of God. Have you known a friend who speaks about the Lord easily and whose prayers are filled with Scripture? Have you sensed that she walks closely with the Lord? Most likely, her knowledge of God and her love for him have grown out of spending significant time in the word. On the pages of Scripture, she's seen and heard the Lord. There she's found him to be merciful, gracious, patient, loving, faithful, and forgiving (Ex. 34:6–7). Likewise, as we read and study the Bible, we will grow in understanding who God is and what he's like. Do you want to have a vibrant faith? Consistently seek to know the Lord in his word.

Second, Scripture sanctifies us. As God instructs us in his word about who he is, he also instructs us about who we are and who we're becoming: we're children of God being conformed to the image of Christ. The apostle Peter explains, "But as he who called you is holy, you also be holy in all your conduct" (1 Pet. 1:15). God applies the truth of Scripture to our lives so that we become more holy in heart and conduct like Jesus. The word teaches us to battle sin: "I have stored up your word in my heart, that I might not sin against you" (Ps. 119:11). It also shows us how to obey:

"I have chosen the way of faithfulness; I set your rules before me" (Ps. 119:30). As we saturate our hearts and minds with the truth of God's word, we will increasingly overcome sin and grow in Christlike obedience.

Third, Scripture makes us wise. God's word is able to make us wise for salvation (2 Tim. 3:15). It also provides us with instruction, guidance, and discernment for daily living (Prov. 1:2–3). God's thoughts and ways are higher than ours, but as we read and meditate on his word, our thoughts and ways become more like his. We learn to discern truth from error and to make choices according to the commands and principles of Scripture. Day by day, our foolishness is replaced with God's wisdom, which is pure, peaceable, gentle, reasonable, merciful, impartial, and sincere (James 3:17).

Fourth, Scripture encourages us. Sometimes it's the small, mundane things of life that can weigh us down, and at other times significant needs or difficult circumstances may discourage and trouble us deeply. In either case, God's word provides us with truth about his presence, promises, and character to help us persevere through any hardship. Scripture gives us hope: "I rise before dawn and cry for help; I hope in your words" (Ps. 119:147). It comforts us: "This is my comfort in my affliction, that your promise gives me life" (Ps. 119:50). And it makes us spiritually strong: "My soul melts away for sorrow; strengthen me according to your word" (Ps. 119:28). In times of trial, God's word fortifies our faith and enables us to endure.

Lastly, Scripture brings blessing into our lives. Every good thing we enjoy is a gift from God and a result of his lovingkindness. Even the blessings we receive by ordering our lives according to his word are by his grace: "Blessed is everyone who fears the LORD, who walks in his ways! You shall eat the fruit of the labor of your hands; you shall be blessed, and it shall be well with you" (Ps. 128:1–2). For example, when we follow Scripture's teaching about finances, we can enjoy freedom from debt. When we apply biblical principles of forgiveness, we can build loving, peaceful relationships. When we commit ourselves to purity and honesty, we can sleep peacefully and enjoy a clear conscience. When we sow the truth of God's word into our lives, we reap the beautiful fruit it produces: "This blessing has fallen to me, that I have kept your precepts" (Ps. 119:56).

Handling the Word of Truth

To encourage your confidence in God's word, in this chapter we've given thought to four key characteristics of Scripture—authority, inerrancy, clarity, and sufficiency—and several ways the word continually transforms our lives as believers. In light of these things, we leave you with four general principles to help guide you as you speak God's truth into the lives of those you love.

1. *Study God's word for yourself.* "Do your best to present yourself to God as one approved, a worker who has no need to be ashamed, rightly handling the word of truth" (2 Tim. 2:15). Devote yourself to the study of Scripture. Learn to carefully observe, understand, and apply it to your own life. You will never be able to freely give to others what you do not possess yourself. As you grow in your knowledge of Scripture, you'll become better equipped to help others with God's word as well.[5]

2. *Don't add anything to God's word.* Jesus said, "This people honors me with their lips, but their heart is far from me; in vain do they worship me, teaching as doctrines the commandments of men" (Mark 7:6–7). When speaking God's truth to another, focus on sharing what Scripture specifically says about her situation. Beware of giving her your own personal opinions and suggestions as if they're the

ultimate answers to her problems. Always point her to Scripture. The transforming wisdom your loved one needs is found in the word of God—not in you, social media, or even helpful books.

3. *Don't take anything away from God's word.* "Whoever relaxes one of the least of these commandments and teaches others to do the same will be called least in the kingdom of heaven, but whoever does them and teaches them will be called great in the kingdom of heaven" (Matt. 5:19). If you find that God's word provides something needful for someone you love, resist the temptation to hold back from sharing it out of fear that she might disagree or be offended. Instead, commit yourself to avoid minimizing or compromising what the Bible teaches. Pray for courage and opportunity to speak the full truth about the gospel and any other issue that needs to be addressed.

4. *Trust the Lord to use his word as he intends.* God's word is powerful to accomplish his good and wise purposes in your life and the lives of those you love. The Lord said, "So shall my word be that goes out from my mouth; it shall not return to me empty, but it shall accomplish that which I purpose, and shall succeed in the thing for which I sent it" (Isa. 55:11). You can't see all that God is doing, but you can know that he's at work, using Scripture both to save and sanctify his people. Be confident in the Lord and in his word to transform lives.

REFLECTION QUESTIONS

1. Read Psalm 19:7–11 and make two lists from this passage. First, list how Scripture is described. Second, list how Scripture transforms us. How has Scripture specifically transformed you?

2. What four attributes of Scripture are described in this chapter? Reread the Bible verses that support each of them and explain each attribute in your own words. What other attributes could be included?

3. What are the five ways Scripture works in believers, as discussed in this chapter? Which of these is the most meaningful to you and why? In what other ways can Scripture impact our lives?

4. Describe your current intake of God's word. How can you increase your knowledge and understanding of Scripture? In addition to attending your church's weekly worship service, consider attending an adult Sunday school class, joining a weekly Bible study, following a Bible reading plan, studying a book of the Bible, or memorizing and meditating on Scripture. Choose at least one of these to begin implementing in your life. Who can you invite to join you?

5. How has this chapter encouraged your confidence in God's word to transform lives? Over this coming week, read all of Psalm 119 and notice the psalmist's confidence in God's word. How can confidence in God's word change how you share it with others?

PART 2

WE'VE COVERED A LOT of ground in this book so far, from understanding God's plan for us to speak his truth to one another, to exploring how God's grace informs how we speak with grace, to reminding ourselves of Scripture's power to transform lives. Now we come to this crucial question: "Where exactly can I turn in the Bible and what biblical truth can I give to someone who needs godly encouragement or counsel?" The rest of this book answers that question.

In the following chapters you will find Scripture passages you can share with those who are worried (chapter 7), weary (chapter 8), wayward (chapter 9), or weeping (chapter 10). Each chapter contains three or four Scripture passages with short explanations of key truths that you can easily communicate to others in their time of need. We've crafted the explanations to read as if you're addressing your loved one directly. Following are some practical suggestions for using these scriptures in your own conversations.

1. *Mark the Scripture passages in your Bible and make a "cheat sheet."* Underline or highlight the key passages in your Bible. Then make a separate cheat sheet listing common struggles (such as "worried," "weary," "weeping," and "wayward") with their corresponding Bible verse references and key ideas so you can quickly remind yourself where to turn in the Scriptures and what biblical truths to share. Write your cheat sheet on the front or back blank pages of your Bible or keep it on your phone along with a Bible app for quick reference. We also recommend that you regularly add relevant verses to this list as you read your Bible and listen to sermons.

2. *Memorize key verses (or at least their references).* There's nothing like good old-fashioned memorization. One of the best ways to memorize these passages is to spend time studying and meditating on them for your own spiritual edification. "Own" these Scripture passages personally, and you'll be better prepared to share them and the truths they contain straight from your heart.

3. *Ask something like this: "May I share with you what the Lord has taught me from the Bible that might help you too?"* Be careful to discern and respect another person's receptivity to hearing Scripture. You can't force your friend to receive the word of God, but the Holy Spirit can prompt her to listen in his perfect timing. If she says no, trust the Lord for a future opportunity. If she says yes, share one Scripture passage you believe would be helpful and meaningful in her situation.

4. *Ask your friend to read the Bible passage.* When possible, have her read the Scripture verses aloud. It's important for others to verbalize, hear, and process the word of God for themselves. Stopping your conversation for a few minutes to let someone carefully

read aloud and consider God's word can make a significant impact on a troubled soul.

5. *If you find it helpful, read the explanations of various Scripture passages directly from this book.* You don't have to look like a know-it-all! And you don't have to be a memory master! Personally, we often refer to and use other biblical resources to give us confidence and direction in our conversations with others. This also helps us to remember key truths that we may otherwise forget.

6. *Use the Bible verses and the explanations in these chapters as starting points for further conversation.* Our biblical explanations aren't intended to be scripts for you to follow exactly. We know that no two conversations are alike. Some conversations are short and others are long. Some scratch the surface and some go deep. Some conversations stay on topic while others go where you never expected. You may have opportunities to discuss a Scripture passage point by point, but you may be led to other verses and truths based upon the need of the moment.

7. *Suggest additional helps from the Recommended Resources list at the back of this book to reinforce the biblical truth you have already discussed.* You can encourage your friend to read these resources on her own. Better yet, you might consider providing her with ongoing support and accountability by working through one of the resources together.

8. *Above all, pray.* Pray for your loved one's spiritual needs and her receptivity to God's word. Pray for God-ordained opportunities to speak truth into her life. Pray for wisdom and humility to saturate your attitude, words, and behavior as you share the Scriptures with her.

7

Truth for the Worried

Humble yourselves, therefore, under the mighty hand of
God so that at the proper time he may exalt you, casting
all your anxieties on him, because he cares for you.

1 PETER 5:6–7

MARIA AND I (CAROLINE) met several years ago at a women's church retreat. She was a young professional who had recently graduated from a prestigious university and obtained a fantastic position in her career field. Always stylish and smiling, Maria appeared to have it all together. I had no idea about her inner turmoil until she told me about it a few Saturday mornings later as we visited at a Starbucks.

Maria admitted she was consumed with worry. She worried about everything, from the most mundane to the more significant issues in her life. Maria began her mornings stressing over what to wear to work: "Is this skirt too short? Is this other one too long? If I wear short sleeves, I might get cold. I could bring my sweater, but does it look okay with this shirt?" A few outfits later, she'd rush out the door, late for the day.

On her commute, Maria wondered if she could meet her boss's expectations: "What if he's upset with my work and I lose my job? How will I pay my bills?" Her mind often jumped to the more imaginary concerns: "Will I have to move out of the area to find work? If I do, I won't be able to watch my nephews grow up. How would I start over somewhere else?"

On top of that, Maria hadn't been feeling well for the past month. When she looked up her symptoms on the Internet, her concerns only increased: "Should I make a doctor's appointment? What if I have a serious condition? If I get really sick and can't work, how will I support myself?"

After encouraging Maria to see her doctor, I asked her a few more questions. I learned these worries were just the tip of the iceberg. Maria told me her mind felt like a cluttered closet. It was filled with so much worry that there wasn't room for much else. She explained, "I barely make it through the day anymore. My work and relationships are suffering. At night, I sit in front of the TV for hours just to escape my thoughts." Her eyes welled up with tears and she continued, "I'm afraid it'll never change."

Even though I hadn't walked in Maria's shoes, I knew what it was like to be anxious and fearful. I could understand her hopelessness and the desire to break free from worry. I could sympathize and listen to Maria, but I also wanted to help her overcome her anxiety. I felt so inadequate in the moment, but I knew God had the answers to her problems. If we could read some relevant scripture together and talk about what it means, it would give her God's wisdom and comfort—even though I was at a loss for words. As Maria looked down at our table and nervously folded a napkin, I reached for my Bible. My mind began to race as I wondered where I should turn in the word to encourage my struggling friend. I decided on Philippians 4:4–9. Months later, Maria would tell me that her healing began that very morning.

Worry by Any Other Name

In Shakespeare's *Romeo and Juliet*, Juliet mused, "What's in a name? That which we call a rose by any other name would smell as sweet." The same is true about worry. Although it's often called by other names, worry by any other name is still worry. Sometimes we describe a worried person as anxious, fearful, obsessed, or panicked. Or we might use a more palatable word such as apprehensive, uneasy, fretful, or bothered. Regardless of the word one uses, to be worried basically means to be overly concerned, distressed, or agitated about something anticipated or about to happen.[1] The worried person, on some level, is fearful about unknown or future circumstances. Whether she's concerned about something actual or imagined, her worrisome thoughts and feelings are very real.

I (Cheryl) used to think that worrying was beyond my control. Of course, I didn't always call it worry. I was "stressed out" or "overwhelmed," and I assumed it was a natural and justified response to my circumstances. But then I had to come to grips with what God clearly says about worry: "Do not fret; it leads only to evildoing" (Ps. 37:8 NASB). The message was clear: I was commanded not to worry, and if I did worry, things would only get worse. Worrying had become such a habit that it seemed impossible to stop. But when God gives his children a command to obey, he also gives what we need in order to obey it. I found exactly what I needed to hear and do in 1 Peter 5:6–7: "*Humble yourselves,* therefore, under the mighty hand of God so that at the proper time he may exalt you, *casting all your anxieties on him,* because he cares for you."

As I considered these and other Bible verses about trusting God, I grew in understanding his loving, sovereign care and the importance of entrusting my concerns to him. Here Peter instructs us to cast, or throw, our worries on the Lord because he cares for us. Often when we say we "care" for someone, we mean we have favorable or compassionate feelings toward that person. But God's care for us isn't merely an attitude or emotion. His care is his wise and kind governance of our lives for our good. He *actively* cares for us in time and space—in every moment and in every circumstance. As I learned to confess my worry to the Lord, to lay my anxieties before him in prayer, and to submit my thoughts to his word, the Lord grew my hope and trust in him, one concern at a time.

In the previous chapter, we discussed how Scripture transforms us. It's now time to get practical about what to say to others from God's life-changing word to help them in their time of need. On the following pages of this chapter, we provide three Bible passages with key points and basic explanations, written as if addressed *directly to the one who is worried.* Choose one or more of these passages to share with or read to your worried friend or loved one, and discuss the main points and explanations with her as you have the opportunity. But first, if you haven't yet read the suggestions at the beginning of part 2, we recommend that you go back and read those suggestions for how to share these verses with others. So now let's look together at God's truth for the worried. We pray that these scriptures will encourage you as well.

Jesus Speaks to the Worried

Therefore I tell you, do not be anxious about your life, what you will eat or what you will drink, nor about your body, what you will put on. Is not life more than food, and the body more than clothing? Look at the birds of the air: they neither sow nor reap nor gather into barns, and yet your heavenly Father feeds them. Are you not of more value than they? And which of you by being anxious can add a single hour to his span of life? And why are you anxious about clothing? Consider the lilies of the field, how they grow: they neither toil nor spin, yet I tell you, even Solomon in all his glory was not arrayed like one of these. But if God so clothes the grass of the field, which today is alive and tomorrow is thrown into the oven, will he not much more clothe you, O you of little faith? Therefore do not be anxious, saying, "What shall we eat?" or "What shall we drink?" or "What shall we wear?" For the Gentiles seek after all these things, and your heavenly Father knows that you need them all. But seek first the kingdom of God and his righteousness, and all these things will be added to you. Therefore do not be anxious about tomorrow, for tomorrow will be anxious for itself. Sufficient for the day is its own trouble. (Matt. 6:25–34)

1. Your heavenly Father knows your every need.

Therefore I tell you, do not be anxious about your life, what you will eat or what you will drink, nor about your body, what you will put on. Is not life more than food, and the body more than clothing? . . . For the Gentiles seek after all these things, and your heavenly Father knows that you need them all. (vv. 25, 32)

In this portion of the Sermon on the Mount, Jesus speaks to the worried. Just as he explained to those who heard his message long ago, Jesus tells you not to be anxious, for your heavenly Father is intimately acquainted with your every need. He loves you, he sees you, and he understands the concerns that burden you. Your gracious and powerful Father knows exactly what you need and will provide whatever is necessary in every circumstance of your life. You're never out of his sight or beyond the reach of his care. Don't be anxious about your needs or frantically strive to meet them. Be still and know that your God is worthy of *all* your trust. You and your every need are known by him.

2. God cares for his smallest creatures, and he cares for you even more.

> Look at the birds of the air: they neither sow nor reap nor gather into barns, and yet your heavenly Father feeds them. Are you not of more value than they? . . . But if God so clothes the grass of the field, which today is alive and tomorrow is thrown into the oven, will he not much more clothe you, O you of little faith? (vv. 26, 30)

Consider for a moment how God cares for the most insignificant of his creatures. The birds always have enough food, and the flowers are always beautifully dressed. Yet you, his precious child, are much more valuable to God. If he provides everything his lesser creatures need, won't he faithfully provide all that you need? Yes! The Lord is your mighty Creator and sustainer, and he's worthy of your wholehearted trust. If you're struggling with worry, remember how he's provided for you in the past and recognize the numerous ways he's providing for you today. Pray for a strong faith to trust him to care for you, even as he cares for all his precious creation.

3. Instead of giving yourself to worry, prioritize and pursue the things of God.

> Therefore do not be anxious, saying, "What shall we eat?" or "What shall we drink?" or "What shall we wear?" . . . But seek first the kingdom of God and his righteousness, and all these things will be added to you. (vv. 31, 33)

Not only does Jesus tell you not to worry, but he also instructs you about what to do instead: seek first God's kingdom and his righteousness. Make the pursuit of God—his glory, his purposes, his holiness—the number-one priority in your life. This begins with your salvation. Have you repented of your sins and trusted in Christ as your Savior? It continues with your devotion to him. Are you now following the Lord in faith and obedience? It means you're delighting in God instead of this world. Are you growing in your love for him, learning to love him with all your heart, soul, mind, and strength? You'll only be satisfied when your soul is filled with what it truly needs: God himself. As you seek the Lord, he'll meet that greatest need and all others besides.

4. Worry can't change anything, so entrust your tomorrows to God.

> And which of you by being anxious can add a single hour to his span of life? . . . Therefore do not be anxious about tomorrow, for tomorrow will be anxious for itself. Sufficient for the day is its own trouble. (vv. 27, 34)

Worry doesn't solve any problems, and it can't change what tomorrow holds. You have enough to care about today, so diligently attend to whatever God has given you to do. Although you can reasonably plan and prepare for tomorrow, you'll never be able to control it.

Tomorrow's problems will work out according to the good and kind providence of the Lord, so lay aside the worry that's weighing you down and sapping your strength. Your future is in the hands of your loving heavenly Father, and you can trust him with it. To overcome your worries about tomorrow, obediently fulfill today's responsibilities, and also fill your mind with Bible verses that remind you of God's faithfulness. With his help, you can learn to welcome each new day—and patiently await each tomorrow—with a trusting heart.

Worry's Remedy

Rejoice in the Lord always; again I will say, rejoice. Let your reasonableness be known to everyone. The Lord is at hand; do not be anxious about anything, but in everything by prayer and supplication with thanksgiving let your requests be made known to God. And the peace of God, which surpasses all understanding, will guard your hearts and your minds in Christ Jesus. Finally, brothers, whatever is true, whatever is honorable, whatever is just, whatever is pure, whatever is lovely, whatever is commendable, if there is any excellence, if there is anything worthy of praise, think about these things. What you have learned and received and heard and seen in me—practice these things, and the God of peace will be with you. (Phil. 4:4–9)

1. Rejoice in the Lord.

Rejoice in the Lord always; again I will say, rejoice. (v. 4)

How can you overcome worry? Begin by rejoicing in the Lord. Perhaps you're wondering, "But how can I rejoice when I'm so unhappy?" You can, because joy is different from happiness. Happiness is a positive emotional response when things are going well, but joy is the attitude of a glad, settled heart that knows *all* will be well in the Lord, regardless of one's circumstances. It's a deep-seated trust in God—believing he's good, sovereign, and faithful—and a confidence that he'll care for you no matter what. Battle your worry by rejoicing in the goodness of God. Worship him for who he is and what he's done. Praise him for his character and promises. Glorify him for his presence and work in your life. Recount everything about the Lord that fills your heart with love and gratitude, and praise him for it! Although your circumstances change, the Lord never will. He's always trustworthy and at hand to care for you. Rejoice in *him*.

2. Pray about what worries you.

Do not be anxious about anything, but in everything by prayer and supplication with thanksgiving let your requests be made known to God. And the peace of God, which surpasses all understanding, will guard your hearts and your minds in Christ Jesus. (vv. 6–7)

In addition to rejoicing in the Lord, overcome your worries with prayer. Your mind is always active, and you can't displace anxious thoughts without prayerfully expressing your dependence on God. Committing your concerns to the Lord in prayer is the way he's provided to guard your heart and mind from further sin and despair. As you humbly bring your requests to the Lord, be specific, thorough, and persistent (Luke 18:1–8). Ask him to do his perfect will in your life, not only working in your circumstances but also molding you into a vessel of strong and unwavering faith. Above all, give thanks to the Lord for his help and faithfulness in your time of trouble. Thank him for this opportunity to be made more like Christ and praise him in advance for his answers to your prayers as you trust him to do what's best.

3. Think about what is good and true.

Finally, brothers, whatever is true, whatever is honorable, whatever is just, whatever is pure, whatever is lovely, whatever is commendable, if there is any excellence, if there is anything worthy of praise, think about these things. (v. 8)

Worry is a monster that must be fed to survive and starved to die. It's fed by fearful, doubting thoughts that often question the future and assume the worst. To put worry to death, identify your anxious thoughts and replace them with thoughts that honor God. Pinpoint the specific lies, half-truths, and speculations you repeatedly tell yourself, and boldly reply to them with truth from God's word. With Spirit-empowered self-control, actively put off the lies that feed your anxiety and put on the thoughts that build your faith. Ponder what is true about God and his word. Think on what is honorable (worthy of respect), just (righteous), pure (clean), lovely (pleasing), commendable (of good repute), excellent (virtuous), and worthy of praise. As you take every thought captive to Christ, worry will begin to wither and peace will begin to grow. (You may find it helpful to write a list of your anxious thoughts with corresponding God-honoring statements and Bible verses that you can refer to throughout the day or night.)

4. Put these things—rejoicing, praying, and thinking rightly—into practice, and you will have peace.

What you have learned and received and heard and seen in me—practice these things, and the God of peace will be with you. (v. 9)

Overcoming worry takes practice. Like an athlete who repeatedly drills a particular skill in order to master it, we need to continually do the things found in Philippians 4:4–9 to gain victory over anxiety. Paul, who wrote this letter to the believers in Philippi, encouraged them to be strong in their faith by putting into practice what he'd taught and modeled with his life. Likewise, you can learn to trust the Lord in any situation as you put Paul's instructions into practice day by day and sometimes even minute by minute. To battle and have victory over anxiety, practice these things: rejoice in the Lord, pray instead of worry, and purposefully think on what is good and true. Then you will experience the genuine peace that's found in God alone.

Turning from Worry to God

The LORD is my light and my salvation;
　　whom shall I fear?
The LORD is the stronghold of my life;
　　of whom shall I be afraid?

When evildoers assail me
　　to eat up my flesh,
my adversaries and foes,
　　it is they who stumble and fall.

Though an army encamp against me,
　　my heart shall not fear;
though war arise against me,
　　yet I will be confident.

One thing have I asked of the LORD,
　　that will I seek after:
that I may dwell in the house of the LORD
　　all the days of my life,

to gaze upon the beauty of the LORD
 and to inquire in his temple.

For he will hide me in his shelter
 in the day of trouble;
he will conceal me under the cover of his tent;
 he will lift me high upon a rock.

And now my head shall be lifted up
 above my enemies all around me,
and I will offer in his tent
 sacrifices with shouts of joy;
I will sing and make melody to the LORD.

Hear, O LORD, when I cry aloud;
 be gracious to me and answer me!
You have said, "Seek my face."
My heart says to you,
 "Your face, LORD, do I seek."
 Hide not your face from me.
Turn not your servant away in anger,
 O you who have been my help.
Cast me not off; forsake me not,
 O God of my salvation!
For my father and my mother have forsaken me,
 but the LORD will take me in.

Teach me your way, O LORD,
 and lead me on a level path
 because of my enemies.

Give me not up to the will of my adversaries;
 for false witnesses have risen against me,
 and they breathe out violence.

I believe that I shall look upon the goodness of the LORD
 in the land of the living!
Wait for the LORD;
 be strong, and let your heart take courage;
 wait for the LORD! (Ps. 27:1–14)

1. The Lord is your salvation—look to him.
The LORD is my light and my salvation;
 whom shall I fear?
The LORD is the stronghold of my life;
 of whom shall I be afraid? . . .

Though an army encamp against me,
 my heart shall not fear;
though war arise against me,
 yet I will be confident. (vv. 1, 3)

An old hymn says, "Turn your eyes upon Jesus; look full in his wonderful face, and the things of earth will grow strangely dim in the light of his glory and grace."[2] The psalmist's example in Psalm 27 reminds you to do the same thing to overcome your worry: look to the Lord. He's your light, your salvation, and the stronghold of your life. You are safe in him both now and forever. The concerns that consume your thoughts can easily draw your attention away from God's character and care for you, especially in your salvation. Since he has met your greatest need of reconciling you to himself through Christ, won't he also meet your every other need? As you have trusted the Lord to be your spiritual stronghold, trust him to be your stronghold in every other circumstance, no matter how dire it seems. You have *nothing* to fear, because you have the Lord—and he certainly has you.

2. The Lord is your shelter—seek him.

One thing have I asked of the LORD,
    that will I seek after:
that I may dwell in the house of the LORD
    all the days of my life,
to gaze upon the beauty of the LORD
    and to inquire in his temple.

For he will hide me in his shelter
    in the day of trouble. . . .

And I will offer in his tent
    sacrifices with shouts of joy;
I will sing and make melody to the LORD. . . .

You have said, "Seek my face."
My heart says to you,
    "Your face, LORD, do I seek." (vv. 4–6, 8)

The psalmist said there was only *one thing* he longed for: to live each day in the presence of God. Even in the worst of circumstances, his ultimate prayer and purpose were to seek the Lord, to know God and to fellowship with him. In your time of trouble, make this your own prayer and purpose as well. Instead of spinning your wheels with worry, give full attention to your relationship with God.

He calls you to seek his face, and as you draw near to him, he'll draw near to you. To seek the Lord, be devoted to prayer, read and meditate on Scripture, obey his word, and worship him with joy. As you delight in the Lord, he'll protect you from the onslaught of worry. In the shelter of his presence, you'll see the beauty of the Lord, and he will cause your faith to flourish.

3. The Lord is your helper—cry out to him.

> Hear, O LORD, when I cry aloud;
>> be gracious to me and answer me! . . .
>> Hide not your face from me.
> Turn not your servant away in anger,
>> O you who have been my help.
> Cast me not off; forsake me not,
>> O God of my salvation!
> For my father and my mother have forsaken me,
>> but the LORD will take me in.
>
> Teach me your way, O LORD,
>> and lead me on a level path
>> because of my enemies. (vv. 7, 9–11)

Where do you turn for help when you're worried? Do you primarily turn to other people for comfort, to activities or addictive substances for distractions, or even to yourself for figuring out how to handle everything on your own? There's only one who's truly *able* to assist you. The Lord alone is infinitely wise, good, and powerful to help you with all your concerns. He promises never to fail or abandon you, even if those closest to you forsake you. So, like the psalmist, cry out to the Lord, your faithful helper. First, ask him to be gracious to you and to answer your prayer in your time of need. Second, ask the Lord to teach you and lead you on the level path of trusting and obeying him as you encounter the challenges that lie ahead. And remember that the Lord will be with you wherever you go.

4. The Lord is good—wait for him.

I believe that I shall look upon the goodness of the LORD
   in the land of the living!
Wait for the LORD;
   be strong, and let your heart take courage;
wait for the LORD! (vv. 13–14)

God's timetable is rarely the same as ours. We often worry about things that are yet to happen, and if we don't see him take care of our concerns as quickly as we like, we may worry even more. In such times, it's tempting to think that the Lord is unloving or uninvolved, but nothing could be further from the truth. God is good, he does good, and he's working all things together for your good. You can't tell the Lord how to care for you, but you can trust that he always will. Wait for him to work in your life, believing that you'll see the goodness of the Lord. As you wait and remind yourself how trustworthy he is, the Lord will give you strength and courage to persevere. Let the knowledge of his goodness toward you dispel your worry and fill you with a steadfast faith.

REFLECTION QUESTIONS

1. Spend time rereading and thoroughly familiarizing yourself with the scriptures and key points presented in this chapter.

2. Which of these Bible passages is the most meaningful to you and why? What does it teach you about God? What does it teach you about yourself? How might it impact what you believe or how you live?

3. Is there another Bible passage or verse that the Lord has used in your life to help you overcome worry? What truth have you personally learned from it that you could share with a worried friend?

4. Read Psalm 34. Underline five verses in this psalm that you think would be an encouragement to someone who is worried. Make your own notes about what those verses say about trusting God.

5. "Anxiety in a man's heart weighs him down, but a good word makes him glad" (Prov. 12:25). Do you know someone who's worried to whom you can give a "good word" this week? Pray for your friend, and whether it be in a conversation or a written note, share with her a relevant Scripture passage from this chapter. Encourage your friend with God's truth in love.

8

Truth for the Weary

And let us not grow weary of doing good, for in
due season we will reap, if we do not give up.

GALATIANS 6:9

MANDY, A YOUNG MOTHER of three who attends my (Caroline's)
church, recently called me saying she needed to talk with an older
mom who could understand her situation. Although she felt awkward asking for advice, she explained that her concerned husband
had urged her to call me, so she finally did. Mandy was utterly
exhausted. She didn't think she had the mental or physical energy,
much less the spiritual strength, to care for her family. Mandy's
children are young and close in age, requiring her constant attention. In addition, Mandy is overwhelmed by the responsibilities of
managing her home during this stage of motherhood. There seems
to be no end or rest in sight.

Mandy's nights are often interrupted by changing sheets for a
child who still wets the bed or by comforting another who doesn't

sleep well. Her youngest won't let her take a shower without crying at the bathroom door. The middle one has a temper and needs to be watched carefully when playing with the other children. Mandy's oldest, a second-grader, is often uncooperative, already isolating himself behind an electronic device. And then there are the mounds of laundry, the constant messes, and the preparation of meals for picky eaters. It all feels like too much.

"I didn't expect motherhood to be so hard," Mandy said quietly. "I feel strung out with nothing to give. I want to be a good mom, but each day ends with regret, guilt, and exhaustion. I don't think I have it in me to do this." By now Mandy was close to tears: "I don't have any 'me' time. It's like I'm shriveling up, and as much as I love my kids, I don't think I can cope anymore."

Although my own three boys are grown, I can remember what it's like to be in Mandy's shoes as if it were yesterday. Sometimes when you're a young mother, the world narrows down to the four walls of your house. Current events and trends in the culture occur without notice. You rarely feel like you've done enough, even though you're busy from morning to night. A few moments alone become a cherished commodity, and having an adult conversation can be surprisingly uplifting.

Mandy asked me for some helpful tips. I gave her a few practical suggestions that could make her days and nights run more smoothly, but I also knew she required spiritual encouragement as well. Instead of platitudes and motivational clichés, Mandy needed the hope and strength that only God through his word can provide—something solid to hold onto and remember when she was weary. Before we got off the phone, I read Isaiah 40:27–31 to Mandy and shared with her what the Lord had taught me from those verses about persevering in my own weariness. Mandy was grateful for the encouragement, and after I prayed for her on the phone, we set up a time for me to stop by to talk with her more the following week.

Uphold the Weary

As you know, mothers of young children aren't the only ones who become weary. At some point, everyone experiences a prolonged and burdensome situation that seems to push the limits of what the body or spirit—or both—can endure. A friend of yours awakes every morning with chronic pain. Your cousin faces another round of chemotherapy. A coworker juggles a couple of jobs, trying to make ends meet for herself and her children. A middle-aged neighbor cares for a disabled child or an elderly parent. A senior citizen restarts motherhood by taking in her neglected grandchildren. Maybe you have a strained relationship with a family member, and it never seems to get better no matter what you do. In circumstances like these, physical or spiritual weariness can become the norm and a deep discouragement can settle in.

In the Bible, to be *weary* means to be faint, to lose heart, or to be discouraged. As we discussed in a previous chapter, the weary are the fainthearted mentioned in 1 Thessalonians 5:14: "And we urge you, brothers, . . . encourage the fainthearted." We're to come alongside the weary with hope-filled words and compassionate action, not with impatience or thoughtless reprimands. They have a long and difficult road to travel, a lengthy test of faith. Serve them with love, cover them with prayer, and fortify them with truth from God's word.

Weariness is not sin, yet it's tempting to respond sinfully to God, others, and our circumstances when we're weary. Our defenses against sin are weakened, and we feel the strong downward pull of worry, anger, selfishness, or despair. But as children of a kind and loving heavenly Father, we must remember that he hasn't left us alone in our weariness. We have Christ who identifies and sympathizes with our weaknesses, and through him we approach the throne of grace for help in our time of need (Heb. 4:15–16).

From that throne of grace, God fulfills his promise to help us endure any hardship that comes our way: "God is faithful, and he will not let you be [tested] beyond your ability, but with the [testing] he will also provide the way of escape, *that you may be able to endure it*" (1 Cor. 10:13). Endurance is the "ability to remain under tremendous weight and pressure without succumbing."[1] It's a patient perseverance that's produced in us by the Spirit of God. The Lord uses our trials and weariness to build our endurance, to refine our character, to teach us to hope, and to assure us of his love (Rom. 5:3–5). These are the spiritual blessings given to the weary one who trusts in him. They are the fruit that grows in the heart pruned by trials and watered with the word.

The rest of this chapter contains three Bible passages with key points and basic explanations, written as if addressed *directly to the one who is weary*. Choose one or more of these Scripture passages to share with or read to your wearied friend or loved one, and discuss the main points and explanations with her as you have the opportunity. In addition, share with her what God has taught you and how you've grown spiritually through your own seasons of weariness. With God's word and a personal testimony of his faithfulness, encourage her to persevere (Gal. 6:9).

Strength for the Weary

Why do you say, O Jacob,
and speak, O Israel,

"My way is hidden from the LORD,
 and my right is disregarded by my God"?
Have you not known? Have you not heard?
The LORD is the everlasting God,
 the Creator of the ends of the earth.
He does not faint or grow weary;
 his understanding is unsearchable.
He gives power to the faint,
 and to him who has no might he increases strength.
Even youths shall faint and be weary,
 and young men shall fall exhausted;
but they who wait for the LORD shall renew their strength;
 they shall mount up with wings like eagles;
they shall run and not be weary;
 they shall walk and not faint. (Isa. 40:27–31)

1. The Lord sees you in your weariness.
 Why do you say, O Jacob,
 and speak, O Israel,
 "My way is hidden from the LORD,
 and my right is disregarded by my God"? (v. 27)

Like the ancient Israelites torn from their homeland and held captive in faraway Babylon, you may question whether God sees you in your ongoing suffering. Your difficult circumstances may seem impossible and unbearable—like you're barely surviving. Perhaps you wonder, "Does God see what I'm going through? Does he know how hard this is? Does he care about me?" God's compassionate answer is yes. He also understands the weakness of your body and spirit. You aren't hidden from or disregarded by God. He loves you and is with you to provide the strength and perseverance you need.

2. The Lord is full of power and understanding.

> Have you not known? Have you not heard?
> The LORD is the everlasting God,
>   the Creator of the ends of the earth.
> He does not faint or grow weary;
>   his understanding is unsearchable. (v. 28)

Sometimes when you're weary, your troubles might loom so large that you lose sight of God and what you know to be true about him. Take a few moments to meditate on *who* he is: the everlasting God and Creator of all things. He has no beginning and no end, and he spoke everything into existence by the power of his word. This is *your* God. His strength has no limit; he never faints or grows weary. His understanding has no limit; he knows everything, including every detail about you and your suffering. In infinite love and wisdom, the Lord has brought you to this season of life so that his divine power might be displayed in you. Take comfort in remembering that the God of heaven and earth personally knows you and will uphold you in your weariness with his eternal power.

3. The Lord will give you the exact strength you need.

> He gives power to the faint,
>   and to him who has no might he increases strength. (v. 29)

We see in Isaiah 40 that the Lord is your everlasting God and Creator, who never faints or grows weary and whose understanding is unsearchable. And yet there's something more that he wants you to know: he gives power to *you*. When you're weak, the Lord will give you the spiritual strength you need to endure your trials. You can do whatever God calls you to do—persevere in suffering, walk in obedience, be content in every circumstance—with the help he gives. The Lord will fill your weakness with power and your weariness with endurance. When you lack strength, his grace will increase in you all the more: "As the day, so shall the grace be."[2]

4. Your strength will be renewed as you wait for the Lord.

Even youths shall faint and be weary,
    and young men shall fall exhausted;
but they who wait for the LORD shall renew their strength;
    they shall mount up with wings like eagles;
they shall run and not be weary;
    they shall walk and not faint. (vv. 30–31)

When your strength is gone, how can you become strong again? When weariness overtakes you, how can you regain the power to carry on? Wait for the Lord, and he will renew your strength. To *wait for the Lord* means to look to him with a patient and expectant hope for provision or deliverance. It's a waiting that's characterized by prayer for divine help and a confident trust in the Lord that he will be faithful. When you feel weary, wait on him. Find a quiet place, even for a few moments, and ask the Lord to empower you. Susanna Wesley, the mother of nineteen children, including the famous brothers John and Charles, often pulled her long apron over her head to pray before she reentered the busyness of her day. Imagine her exhaustion! Yet God gave her grace to persevere and to do his will.[3] He promises the same to you.

Being Renewed Day by Day

We have this treasure in jars of clay, to show that the surpassing power belongs to God and not to us. We are afflicted in every way, but not crushed; perplexed, but not driven to despair; persecuted, but not forsaken; struck down, but not destroyed; always carrying in the body the death of Jesus, so that the life of Jesus may also be manifested in our bodies. For we who live are always being given over to death for Jesus' sake, so that the life of Jesus also may be manifested in our mortal flesh. So death is at work in us, but life in you. Since we have the same spirit of faith according to what has been written, "I believed, and so I spoke," we also believe, and so we also speak, knowing that he who raised the Lord Jesus will raise us also with Jesus and bring us with you into his presence. For it is all for your sake, so that as grace extends to more and more people it may increase thanksgiving, to the glory of God. So we do not lose heart. Though our outer self is wasting away, our inner self is being renewed day by day. For this light momentary affliction is preparing for us an eternal weight of glory beyond all comparison, as we look not to the things that are seen but to the things that are unseen. For the things that are seen are transient, but the things that are unseen are eternal. (2 Cor. 4:7–18)

1. The strength to endure your trials comes from God, and not from yourself.

We have this treasure in jars of clay, to show that the surpassing power belongs to God and not to us. We are afflicted in every way, but not crushed; perplexed, but not driven to despair; persecuted, but not forsaken; struck down, but not destroyed; always carrying in the body the death of Jesus, so that the life of Jesus may also be manifested in our bodies. (vv. 7–10)

Like a priceless treasure placed into a common jar of clay, God has placed his precious gospel within you. He's filled you with his grace so that Christ's life and power will be manifested, or displayed, in you. Just as your Savior endured many trials, you can also expect to suffer in this world. Even now, you may be afflicted, perplexed, persecuted, or struck down—and so very weary. But take comfort in knowing that your risen Lord is alive in you and will strengthen and protect you through every trial you face. The power you possess is from God and not of yourself. As you depend on him, be assured that he won't allow you to be crushed, driven to despair, forsaken, or destroyed. The indwelling life of his Son will enable you to endure whatever you may suffer.

*2. Place your confidence in God,
knowing that he'll raise you to eternal life.*

Since we have the same spirit of faith according to what has been written, "I believed, and so I spoke," we also believe, and so we also speak, knowing that he who raised the Lord Jesus will raise us also with Jesus and bring us with you into his presence. (vv. 13–14)

In these verses Paul quotes Psalm 116 and explains that he had the same spirit (attitude) of faith as the psalmist. Both Paul and the psalmist possessed a confidence in the Lord that declared his faithfulness even in their suffering. Both of them trusted the Lord because he had shown himself to be trustworthy in their lives time and again. They also trusted him because they knew he was able to deliver their souls from death. Knowing that God is powerful to raise his people to eternal life gave them strength to endure the sufferings of *this* life. Do you long to have a steadfast faith? Do you want to live each day with an unshakable confidence in the Lord despite your circumstances? Then constantly remind yourself that your God, who raised Jesus from the dead and will raise you to eternal life as well, is the same God who promises you his power to persevere today.

3. The future glory that awaits you in heaven far outweighs your present suffering.

So we do not lose heart. Though our outer self is wasting away, our inner self is being renewed day by day. For this light momentary affliction is preparing for us an eternal weight of glory beyond all comparison. (vv. 16–17)

There's no denying that your body is aging. If you haven't sensed it yet, you will! Eventually you'll have more aches and pains and less strength and stamina. Despite the weariness or "wasting away" of your body, God is in the process of renewing your spirit day by day. He's preparing you for heaven by growing you spiritually—in one way or another, bit by bit—to become more holy like his Son. Every trial is an opportunity for godliness, joy, and endurance to be formed in you. Each affliction is producing for you an eternal glory in heaven that far outweighs your present suffering. Compared to the everlasting joy and blessing that await, your present suffering is only light and momentary. Don't lose heart! Keep looking with hope toward the future glory that God is preparing for you.

4. God will give you strength to persevere
as you trust his eternal promises.

> . . . as we look not to the things that are seen but to the things
> that are unseen. For the things that are seen are transient, but
> the things that are unseen are eternal. (v. 18)

It's tempting to put your confidence in what is seen, such as relationships and institutions, money and possessions, health and
vocations. But all these things are temporary. They will pass away
and may even become a source of suffering in your life. Don't look
to them for your ultimate fulfillment and purpose; rather, set your
gaze "beyond the physical to the spiritual, beyond the present to the
future, and beyond the visible to the invisible."[4] Fix your hope, your
complete trust, on your faithful God and his eternal promises in
his word. When this world makes you weary, fortify your soul with
God's everlasting truth, and he will give you strength to persevere
until your faith becomes sight and you see your Savior face to face.

God's Power in Your Weakness

> To keep me [Paul] from becoming conceited because of the
> surpassing greatness of the revelations, a thorn was given me in
> the flesh, a messenger of Satan to harass me, to keep me from
> becoming conceited. Three times I pleaded with the Lord about
> this, that it should leave me. But he said to me, "My grace is
> sufficient for you, for my power is made perfect in weakness."
> Therefore I will boast all the more gladly of my weaknesses,
> so that the power of Christ may rest upon me. For the sake of
> Christ, then, I am content with weaknesses, insults, hardships,
> persecutions, and calamities. For when I am weak, then I am
> strong. (2 Cor. 12:7–10)

1. God is teaching you humility and dependence on him.

A thorn was given me in the flesh, a messenger of Satan to harass me, to keep me from becoming conceited. (v. 7)

When going through a difficult trial, have you wondered, "Why is God allowing this in my life?" It's impossible to fully answer this question because God, in his perfect wisdom, is always working to accomplish good purposes that you can't even imagine. But one thing you can know for certain is that God is using your trial to teach you humility and to root out any pride that may occupy your heart. He's teaching you to wholly depend on him for the strength you need. Like Paul's thorn in the flesh in 2 Corinthians 12, your trial and weariness aren't in vain. God is doing a gracious work in you to make you more like your Savior, who, when he suffered, humbly submitted and entrusted himself to the Father. Although your thorn is painful, it's producing in you the good fruit of Christlike humility and dependence on God. You can trust the Lord that he's doing a good work in you.

2. God's grace is sufficient for you in your time of need.

Three times I pleaded with the Lord about this, that it should leave me. But he said to me, "My grace is sufficient for you." (vv. 8–9)

Paul repeatedly asked the Lord to take away his thorn, yet his thorn remained. Maybe you've asked the Lord to remove your trial, but your circumstances haven't changed either. Be assured that God has not forsaken you. He's with you in your suffering to give you his all-sufficient grace to endure. God's grace isn't an abstract, theological concept. It's his actual help, which he provides by his Spirit in your time of need. His grace is the spiritual power active within you that can only be explained by the presence of the Lord. And his grace is sufficient—perfectly enough and fully adequate—to give you the strength and perseverance your particular trial requires. This mighty grace of God will comfort, uphold, and empower you when your thorn seems impossible to bear.

3. God is perfecting his power in you.

"My power is made perfect in weakness." Therefore I will boast all the more gladly of my weaknesses, so that the power of Christ may rest upon me. (v. 9)

When you recognize your inadequacies—when your strength, abilities, and resources aren't enough to uphold you—you begin to see more clearly your desperate need for the grace, or power, that only God can provide. When you humbly acknowledge how weak you are, that's when Christ's power works mightily within you. As you live in humble dependence on him, his power will be displayed and perfected in you. His strength enables you to live in faith and obedience and to accomplish whatever he has called you to do. The Lord fills up the depth of your weakness with a perfect measure of his strength. So like Paul, you also should glory in your weakness, for only then can you point to Christ and say that *he* has done great things.

4. Be content in your weakness, knowing that Christ is revealing his power in you.

For the sake of Christ, then, I am content with weaknesses, insults, hardships, persecutions, and calamities. For when I am weak, then I am strong. (v. 10)

Paul was content with his weaknesses because he understood them to be for the sake, or honor, of Christ. They were opportunities for Christ's power to be displayed in his life. Instead of chafing against his sufferings, Paul embraced them, knowing that God would give him the strength to endure. Do you see your trials and weariness in this way? Have you learned to be content with your weaknesses, knowing that Christ will make you strong? Have you learned to be content with your weariness, knowing that his grace will be sufficient? Have you learned to be content in all things, knowing that Christ will be glorified? In order to know the power of Christ in your life, acknowledge your frailties and trust him for the supernatural power he promises to provide. In your weariness receive his strength, and Christ will receive the glory.

REFLECTION QUESTIONS

1. Spend time rereading and thoroughly familiarizing yourself with the scriptures and key points presented in this chapter.

2. Which of these Bible passages is the most meaningful to you and why? What does it teach you about God? What does it teach you about yourself? How might it impact what you believe or how you live?

3. Is there another Bible passage or verse that the Lord has used in your own life to strengthen you in your weariness? What truth have you personally learned from it that you could share with a weary friend?

4. Read Psalm 71. Underline five verses in this psalm that you think would be an encouragement to someone who is weary. Make your own notes about what those verses say about trusting God.

5. First Thessalonians 5:11 reminds us to "encourage one another and build one another up, just as you are doing." Do you have a weary friend you can encourage this week? How can you love her in a practical way (such as babysitting, making a meal, or running errands)? Pray for your friend, and whether it be in a conversation or a written note, share with her a relevant Scripture passage from this chapter. Strengthen her with God's truth in love.

9

Truth for the Wayward

Whoever desires to love life and see good days . . .
let him turn away from evil and do good.

I PETER 3:10–11

KELLY AND I (CHERYL) have known each other for what seems like forever. We met at the beginning of middle school, and I have many fun memories of being with Kelly both in school and at youth group activities. After graduating from high school we headed off to different colleges, but we stayed in touch. We even attended each other's weddings and baby showers, but with passing years and cross-country moves we grew apart. Annual Christmas cards and social media kept us informed about each other's lives, and we touched base by phone once a year or so.

A couple of years ago, I received an unexpected call from Kelly's mother. She told me she was very concerned about Kelly, who had recently left her husband. Her children had entered college, and now, despite her husband's desire to preserve the marriage, Kelly had simply told her mother that she was done. To make a long story short, neither of them had committed infidelity or abuse in the marriage, but they did experience conflict, discontent, and bitterness. Kelly had withdrawn from her extended family and church, so her mother asked if I, as a longtime Christian friend, would reach out to Kelly to encourage her any way I could.

I'll be honest. I dreaded contacting Kelly. We weren't particularly close anymore, so why would she want to hear from me? She'd never confided in me about her marriage, so I couldn't imagine that she'd want to talk to me about it now. But I knew that Kelly professed to be a Christian and that no matter what was going on in her life, she needed encouragement to trust and obey the Lord. She needed to know that God loved her and was calling her back to himself and her family. She needed to know God would be faithful to provide the way. Not knowing all the details of Kelly's circumstances, I began praying, "Lord, please teach Kelly whatever she needs to learn. Please restore her marriage, and give me wisdom and grace if I ever have the chance to speak with her."

Over the next couple of months, I tried contacting Kelly a few times by leaving a voicemail or sending a text, but I got no response. I was concerned about her, but I also felt awkward contacting her because it appeared that she didn't want to talk to me. One day I decided to call again, and this time, to my surprise, Kelly answered the phone. Although the conversation was polite, it lasted only a few minutes. I had no opportunity to talk about anything significant before Kelly obviously wanted to get off the phone. Before she hung up, I quickly said, "I care about you, Kelly, but the Lord does even more. I'm praying for you, and I'm here if you ever want to talk."

A few weeks later I was so burdened about Kelly that, despite my fear of being a bother, I called her once again. This time Kelly's voice was different—it wasn't as cold as before. Within a few minutes, she began talking about one of the problems in her marriage and her desire to be happy and independent. She also revealed that an older Christian woman at her new job had been telling her to move back home and work things out with her husband. I took the opportunity to share a Scripture passage and some biblical advice that applied to Kelly's situation. She listened quietly and then said, "Thanks for calling, Cheryl. Let's talk again sometime."

During the next few months, there were several more phone calls between Kelly and me, and often she was the one who called. I would listen, share insights from Scripture, remind her of God's holiness and grace, and pray with her on the phone. In time, as the Spirit changed Kelly's heart through his word, she moved back home to work on her marriage. Kelly and her husband received counsel and discipleship through their church, and eventually their marriage was restored.

Recently, Kelly and I were able to see each other in person. As we visited over dinner, she described her spiritual journey over the past couple of years. Kelly's renewed peace and joy were evident. At one point she asked, "Cheryl, why did you keep on contacting me during those months? You must have known that I didn't want to hear from you." My answer was simple: "Kelly, I just wanted you to know that no matter how far you'd gone, God would always welcome you back."

Pursuing the Wayward

Whenever a believer strays from God and lives in a pattern of sin contrary to God's word, her relationship with her heavenly Father needs to be restored. Nothing, not even her sin, can separate her from the love of God, but her ongoing disobedience dishonors him and brings his discipline. Eventually it will give her reason to examine if her profession of faith in Christ is genuine. When wayward, she needs to be called back to humbly submit to his loving rule in her life, to "lay aside every weight, and sin which clings so closely, and [to] run with endurance the race that is set before [her], looking to Jesus, the founder and perfecter of our faith" (Heb. 12:1–2). You may be the one God uses to pursue her—to admonish her to forsake her sin and to encourage her to grow in Christlikeness.

If you're like us, the thought of talking with someone about her sin and the need to repent before God is uncomfortable at best and terrifying at worst. Few people like to have that kind of conversation, but it may be necessary when another believer in your life is continually sinning in a way that flagrantly violates God's word, shames the name of Christ, and harms herself or others. It can be tempting to ignore her disobedience or to assume that someone else will talk with her about it. You may even wonder if Scripture instructs *you* to speak with her about her sin. The answer is yes. Consider these verses:

> Brothers, if anyone is caught in any transgression, you who are spiritual should restore him in a spirit of gentleness. Keep watch on yourself, lest you too be tempted. (Gal. 6:1)

> If your brother sins against you, go and tell him his fault, between you and him alone. If he listens to you, you have gained your brother. (Matt. 18:15)

> Pay attention to yourselves! If your brother sins, rebuke him, and if he repents, forgive him. (Luke 17:3)

My brothers, if anyone among you wanders from the truth and someone brings him back, let him know that whoever brings back a sinner from his wandering will save his soul from death and will cover a multitude of sins. (James 5:19–20)

There are three principles that we should keep in mind when urging another believer to turn from her sin to obey Christ. First, speak the wisdom of God, not human or worldly wisdom (1 Cor. 2:12–13). Instead of giving merely your own opinion about her sin, show her what God says about it in the Scriptures. Take her to specific Bible passages and examples that address her disobedience. Second, speak with gentleness and love (2 Cor. 2:4). Let affection for your friend and concern for her spiritual well-being guide your words and attitudes in your conversations with her. And, third, speak with the goal of restoration. The hope and aim of addressing another believer's wrongdoing should be to encourage her to repent from sin and to return to a right relationship, first and foremost with God and consequently with others. The purpose is not to bring the wayward hurt or shame (1 Cor. 4:14), but spiritual healing, joy, and restoration through truth and love.[1]

On the next several pages, you'll find four Bible passages with key points and basic explanations written as if addressed *directly to the one who is wayward.* After giving prayerful consideration to the nature of the wayward one's sin and the possible condition of her heart, carefully select one or more of these Scripture passages to share with or read to her, and discuss the main points and explanations with her as you have the opportunity. Although having such conversations can feel uncomfortable and daunting, we can assure you from God's word and our own experiences that the

Lord intends to use loving discussions like these to help restore the wayward to himself.

A Warning and a Blessing

Trust in the LORD with all your heart,
   and do not lean on your own understanding.
In all your ways acknowledge him,
   and he will make straight your paths.
Be not wise in your own eyes;
   fear the LORD, and turn away from evil.
It will be healing to your flesh
   and refreshment to your bones. (Prov. 3:5–8)

1. Wholeheartedly trust in the Lord.

Trust in the LORD with all your heart. . . .
   In all your ways acknowledge him. (vv. 5–6)

Life is full of choices. Some are morally neutral while others are distinctly moral. The latter choices are between what's right and wrong according to God's word. What kind of choices are you making? Do they reveal that you're trusting God? Are you acknowledging by your choices that Christ is your Lord? If your choices contradict God's will for you as revealed in Scripture, then you're not trusting him. As believers we live by faith, which means that we not only trust God for eternal life but we also trust him with our present lives by obeying him, even when it's difficult. The way to trust and acknowledge the Lord is by doing what *he* says is right: by aligning your life with *his* word. Trust him with *all* your heart—with your feelings, intellect, and will. Acknowledge him in *all* your ways—with every choice you make. Trust the Lord that his ways are best for you.

2. Don't be wise in your own eyes.

Do not lean on your own understanding. . . .

Be not wise in your own eyes. (vv. 5, 7)

Apart from knowing and applying God's word to your life by the power of the Spirit, you cannot understand how to live—how God created you to live. The world may tell you to trust and follow your heart, but God tells you to trust and follow him. God warns you to not be wise in your own eyes because your understanding can easily be clouded and lead you into sin. You can be swayed by your emotions, enticed by your desires, influenced by worldly ideals and advice, and even deceived by the enemy. Beware of rationalizing your sin—be careful not to view as good what God says is bad nor what God says is good as bad. And though you may agree with what he says is good, don't fall into the trap of believing your sinful choices are *better* for you because of the circumstances in which you find yourself. Foolishness is trusting your own heart, but wisdom is trusting the heart of God.

3. You'll find blessing if you fear the Lord and turn away from sin.

He will make straight your paths. . . .

Fear the LORD, and turn away from evil.

It will be healing to your flesh

and refreshment to your bones. (vv. 6–8)

If you trust the Lord instead of your own understanding, God will make your path (your course of life) straight or "right, pleasant, prosperous."[2] This doesn't mean that your life will be free of trouble, but it does mean that you'll enjoy the blessings of the Lord's fellowship, care, and guidance as you walk in obedience to him. If you're living in disobedience, give heed to what is commanded in these verses from Proverbs 3. First, fear the Lord. Revere God as holy. Recognize him as the righteous judge who has forgiven your sin and calls you to honor him. Second, turn away from evil. Forsake your sin and pursue what is good and right. Depart from the waywardness and foolishness that is draining you physically and spiritually. Repentance will refresh both your body and your soul as you drink of the Lord's mercy.

Walk by the Spirit

I [Paul] say, walk by the Spirit, and you will not gratify the desires of the flesh. For the desires of the flesh are against the Spirit, and the desires of the Spirit are against the flesh, for these are opposed to each other, to keep you from doing the things you want to do. But if you are led by the Spirit, you are not under the law. Now the works of the flesh are evident: sexual immorality, impurity, sensuality, idolatry, sorcery, enmity, strife, jealousy, fits of anger, rivalries, dissensions, divisions, envy, drunkenness, orgies, and things like these. I warn you, as I warned you before, that those who do such things will not inherit the kingdom of God. But the fruit of the Spirit is love, joy, peace, patience, kindness, goodness, faithfulness, gentleness, self-control; against such things there is no law. And those who belong to Christ Jesus have crucified the flesh with its passions and desires. If we live by the Spirit, let us also keep in step with the Spirit. (Gal. 5:16–25)

1. Examine yourself: Are you walking by the Spirit?

I say, walk by the Spirit, and you will not gratify the desires of the flesh. For the desires of the flesh are against the Spirit, and the desires of the Spirit are against the flesh, for these are opposed to each other, to keep you from doing the things you want to do. (vv. 16–17)

If you're a believer, you have the Spirit of God living in you, empowering you to obey the Lord. To *walk by the Spirit* means to continually and habitually live under the Spirit's control, submitting your life to the teachings of God's word. If you walk by the Spirit, you will not "gratify the desires of the flesh" (v. 16). (*The flesh* refers not only to your body but also to your emotions, mind, and will.) In other words, if you submit yourself to the Spirit of God, you won't continue to live in unrepentant sin. Rather, you will pursue holiness for the honor of Christ. The Spirit and the flesh oppose one another, but they don't have equal power. In Christ, your old self has died, and you're no longer a slave to sin. Your relationship to sin has changed. Its rule over you has been broken, and you can say no to sin. You're now free to obey and glorify Christ through the power of the Spirit living in you.

2. Beware if you're living according to the flesh.

Now the works of the flesh are evident: sexual immorality, impurity, sensuality, idolatry, sorcery, enmity, strife, jealousy, fits of anger, rivalries, dissensions, divisions, envy, drunkenness, orgies, and things like these. I warn you, as I warned you before, that those who do such things will not inherit the kingdom of God. (vv. 19–21)

The sins of the flesh listed in these verses characterize the person who's apart from Christ. If she continues to sin in these ways, it reveals that she doesn't know him, and she won't enter his eternal kingdom. She's under the wrath of God (Rom. 1:18). These sins can be divided into three categories: sins against the body (immorality, impurity, sensuality, drunkenness, orgies); sins against God (idolatry, sorcery); and sins against others (enmity, strife, jealousy, fits of anger, rivalries, dissensions, divisions, envy). If you profess to be a

Christian and yet you persist in any of these sins, understand that you're living in opposition to God. Examine yourself whether you are truly in the faith: do any of these sins control or characterize your life? If so, confess your sin to God and repent. Turn from the sin that entangles you, trust in Christ for forgiveness, and begin walking by the Spirit.

3. If you belong to Christ, keep in step with the Spirit.

The fruit of the Spirit is love, joy, peace, patience, kindness, goodness, faithfulness, gentleness, self-control; against such things there is no law. And those who belong to Christ Jesus have crucified the flesh with its passions and desires. If we live by the Spirit, let us also keep in step with the Spirit. (vv. 22–25)

The Spirit of God produces fruit, or godly attitudes, in the life of every genuine believer. The fruit of the Spirit—love, joy, peace, patience, kindness, goodness, faithfulness, gentleness, and self-control—stands in stark contrast to the sinful deeds of the flesh mentioned in the previous verses. If you belong to Christ through faith, your flesh and its sinful desires have been crucified, and you are now alive to God. Since you've been rescued from the power and penalty of sin and made alive to God by his Spirit, you must no longer seek after sin. Instead, pursue loving obedience to God. Don't give yourself to sinful desires and behavior; rather, give yourself to God to do what pleases him. Cultivate the fruit of the Spirit in your life. Keep in step with him and forsake your sin.

What Is Genuine Repentance?

As it is, I [Paul] rejoice, not because you were grieved, but because you were grieved into repenting. For you felt a godly grief, so that you suffered no loss through us. For godly grief produces a repentance that leads to salvation without regret, whereas worldly grief produces death. For see what earnestness this godly grief has produced in you, but also what eagerness to clear yourselves, what indignation, what fear, what longing, what zeal, what punishment! At every point you have proved yourselves innocent in the matter. (2 Cor. 7:9–11)

1. I'm addressing your sin because I love you,
not because I want to cause you any harm.

As it is, I rejoice, not because you were grieved, but because you were grieved into repenting. For you felt a godly grief, so that you suffered no loss through us. (v. 9)

Just as Paul confronted the sin of the Corinthian believers because of his love for them, I'm addressing your sin because I love you too. I'm concerned for you spiritually. It's not because I think I'm better than you or want to hurt you in any way. Instead, I'm talking with you about this sin in your life because, as followers of Christ, we're to help one another walk with him in faith and obedience. Loving you involves wanting what is best for you, and living in reverent obedience to Christ is always best. If our conversation does cause you grief, my prayer is that your sorrow will lead you to turn away from your sin and turn back to honoring the Lord with your life.

2. Godly grief over sin will lead to repentance and salvation,
but worldly grief will lead only to spiritual death.

Godly grief produces a repentance that leads to salvation without regret, whereas worldly grief produces death. (v. 10)

Godly grief is a sincere sorrow over your sin, produced by the Spirit of God working within you. It's the first step toward repentance, and there can be no repentance without it. This is a sorrow that recognizes you've sinned against God, and it redirects you to Christ, your Savior, as your only hope of forgiveness and restoration. If you turn back to God and his ways, you'll never regret it. Your sorrow before the Lord will turn to joy. On the other hand, worldly grief is a remorse marked by wounded pride, blame-shifting, and frustration or sadness over personal consequences or the loss of sin's fulfillment. It leads to spiritual death, self-pity, shame, and despair. Worldly grief has no hope for overcoming the sin that caused it, but godly grief results in repentance and reconciliation with God and others. Check your heart. Do you grieve over your sin? If so, is it godly or worldly grief?

3. Genuine repentance is a change of mind that involves turning from your sin and pursuing faith-filled obedience toward God.

> See what earnestness this godly grief has produced in you, but also what eagerness to clear yourselves, what indignation, what fear, what longing, what zeal, what punishment! At every point you have proved yourselves innocent in the matter. (v. 11)

You may have heard that repentance is a change of mind or attitude about your sin, a forsaking of sin and a turning toward God. But you may still wonder, "What does genuine repentance look like *practically?*" To describe the Corinthians' heartfelt repentance, Paul used these words: earnestness, eagerness, indignation, fear, longing, zeal, and punishment. They may seem like unusual words to describe repentance, but each of them explains an aspect of repentance that is important for you to understand.[3] True repentance involves:

- an *earnestness* to forsake your sin and to pursue what is good and right;
- an *eagerness* to rebuild your reputation so that it's above reproach and to earn others' trust once again;
- an *indignation* (a righteous anger or hatred) against your own sin and the disgrace it brought on the name of Christ;
- a *fear* (a holy awe or reverence) for God that desires not to displease or dishonor him;
- a *longing* to be restored to God and others you have sinned against;
- a *zeal* (an eagerness or fervor) to do what is right before the Lord and to live for his honor;
- and *punishment,* indicating a desire for justice that humbly accepts the consequences resulting from your sin.

Lastly, Paul describes the Corinthians as "innocent in the matter." In other words, repentance is marked by a renewed purity of heart and life. If you're truly repentant, then you'll delight in your relationship with Christ and pursue personal holiness for his glory.

God's Steadfast Love for the Wayward

Blessed is the one whose transgression is forgiven,
    whose sin is covered.
Blessed is the man against whom the Lord counts no iniquity,
    and in whose spirit there is no deceit.

For when I kept silent, my bones wasted away
    through my groaning all day long.
For day and night your hand was heavy upon me;
    my strength was dried up as by the heat of summer.

I acknowledged my sin to you,
    and I did not cover my iniquity;
I said, "I will confess my transgressions to the LORD,"
    and you forgave the iniquity of my sin.

Therefore let everyone who is godly
    offer prayer to you at a time when you may be found;
surely in the rush of great waters,
    they shall not reach him.
You are a hiding place for me;
    you preserve me from trouble;
    you surround me with shouts of deliverance.

I will instruct you and teach you in the way you should go;
    I will counsel you with my eye upon you.
Be not like a horse or a mule, without understanding,
    which must be curbed with bit and bridle,
    or it will not stay near you.

Many are the sorrows of the wicked,
    but steadfast love surrounds the one who trusts in the LORD.
Be glad in the LORD, and rejoice, O righteous,
    and shout for joy, all you upright in heart! (Ps. 32:1–11)

*1. The Lord mercifully forgives and covers your
sin, and he holds it against you no longer.*
    Blessed is the one whose transgression is forgiven,
        whose sin is covered.
    Blessed is the man against whom the LORD counts no iniquity,
        and in whose spirit there is no deceit. . . .

I acknowledged my sin to you,
and I did not cover my iniquity;
I said, "I will confess my transgressions to the LORD,"
and you forgave the iniquity of my sin. (vv. 1–2, 5)

The Lord is merciful; he doesn't treat you as your sin deserves. The Lord is gracious; he gives you favor that you haven't earned. But he's also just; he punishes sin. Because Jesus bore the wrath of God on the cross for your sin, you're truly blessed. When you trusted in him as your Savior, your sin—past, present, and future—was forgiven, covered, and no longer held against you. You're now free from all condemnation. And yet as long as you're in this world, you'll still sin. You may even wander into grievous sin, yet the Lord remains merciful and forgives. Like the psalmist, in prayer acknowledge and confess (agree with God) that you've sinned against him, and he'll restore you to himself like a loving parent receives a wayward child who returns home.

*2. The Lord delivers you from sin's judgment and
teaches you how to live righteously for him.*

Therefore let everyone who is godly
offer prayer to you at a time when you may be found;
surely in the rush of great waters,
they shall not reach him.
You are a hiding place for me;
you preserve me from trouble;
you surround me with shouts of deliverance.

I will instruct you and teach you in the way you should go;
I will counsel you with my eye upon you. (vv. 6–8)

Don't delay in returning to the Lord. He's speaking to you through his word and calling you to confess and forsake your sin *today*. All sin is worthy of God's just wrath, but be assured of this: no one who seeks refuge in Christ will experience the judgment she deserves. Jesus is your hiding place and strong protector who delivers you from the power of sin in your present life and its eternal consequences in the next. In Christ, you've been set free to pursue righteous living for his sake. As you repent of your sin to walk obediently with him, he promises to instruct, teach, and counsel you in the way you should go. Read and study God's word—fill your heart and mind with his truth—and his Spirit will give you the wisdom and guidance you need to live victoriously over sin (John 17:17).

*3. The Lord surrounds you with his steadfast
love and fills your heart with joy.*

> Many are the sorrows of the wicked,
>> but steadfast love surrounds the one who trusts in the LORD.
> Be glad in the LORD, and rejoice, O righteous,
>> and shout for joy, all you upright in heart! (vv. 10–11)

Sin is deceitful. When sin is chosen, it often seems to be the right thing—no, the *best* thing—to make us happy. But that's an illusion. Sin has consequences that compound with time: broken relationships, unfulfilled expectations, loss of freedoms and opportunities, a guilty conscience, and many other sorrows that can plague one's life. If this is where you now find yourself, understand that this isn't where you must stay. The Lord welcomes you with arms opened wide. He loves you with an everlasting love that cannot be broken. His persevering love surrounds you on every side to protect you from falling away forever and to defend you from the attacks of the enemy. In perfect love, he forgives your sin and gives you every spiritual blessing to walk uprightly with him from the heart. He'll redeem what has been lost and broken in your life and use it to display his glory in you. And in this there's great joy—the joy of forgiveness, the joy of righteousness, the joy of life in Christ. Praise him for his steadfast love!

REFLECTION QUESTIONS

1. Spend time rereading and thoroughly familiarizing yourself with the scriptures and key points presented in this chapter.

2. Which of these Bible passages is the most meaningful to you and why? What does it teach you about God? What does it teach you about yourself? How might it impact what you believe or how you live?

3. First Thessalonians 5:14 (NASB) tells us to "admonish the unruly, encourage the fainthearted, help the weak, be patient with everyone." What other Bible verses or biblical examples can give you guidance as you admonish the unruly? What do your verses or examples teach about the attitude you should have when speaking with the unruly or wayward?

4. Read 2 Corinthians 2:14–17. Describe the analogy that is used in these verses to illustrate your influence on others. What are the two different ways people may respond to you as you represent the knowledge of Christ? What do you learn from these verses about how to call a friend to repentance?

5. James 5:19–20 says: "My brothers, if anyone among you wanders from the truth and someone brings him back, let him know that whoever brings back a sinner from his wandering will save his soul from death and will cover a multitude of sins." Do you know someone who is wandering away from the Lord? Pray for your friend and have a conversation with her that includes a relevant Scripture passage from this chapter. Gently admonish her with God's truth in love.

10

Truth for the Weeping

He will wipe away every tear from their eyes,
and death shall be no more, neither shall there be
mourning, nor crying, nor pain anymore.

REVELATION 21:4

"I'M SO SORRY FOR CRYING." My (Caroline's) new friend, Melanie, could barely get the words out between sobs. Have you ever noticed how often people apologize for weeping? I felt helpless as I sat beside Melanie in my living room, and I certainly didn't think she needed to apologize for expressing her grief. She and her husband, Pete, had recently moved into our area to be near their grandchildren, so they were in the process of making new friends and finding a church. When she and I first met, we realized how much we had in common, and our friendship had grown quickly. Our husbands also enjoyed one another's company, so all four of us regularly spent time together socially.

I was glad that Melanie trusted me enough to share her story with me, even though it was hard to hear. Earlier that week, she'd discovered that Pete had been hiding an affair for quite some time. Having been married for thirty-two years, Melanie could hardly believe what was happening. Sure, she had seen some signs, but she had never expected this. What's worse, after Melanie confronted Pete, he said that he didn't know whether he wanted to remain in the marriage.

Melanie's world was falling apart. She felt so alone. She knew only a few people at the church they'd been visiting, and she didn't feel like talking to a pastor she hardly knew. Melanie's tearful words gushed out of a deep wound: "My world is crashing down around me. I love him. . . . I don't want to be alone for the rest of my life. Pete and I sacrificed and saved and built a life together all these years—and now this?"

Melanie's grief was compounded by the recent death of her elderly mother. In the past, she would turn to her mom whenever things were difficult, and now that source of strength was gone. "I've lost so much, Caroline. What do I do about all this pain inside?" she whispered with her head in her hands. Melanie's story was almost more than I could bear, and my own emotions began to well up inside.

I sat speechless as I processed all that Melanie had said, and I couldn't help but weep with her. It was time to be quiet and cry. It didn't seem right that my sweet friend had to experience such pain and sorrow. The feelings of betrayal, abandonment, and loss were overwhelming. Melanie was a devoted wife who had entrusted so much to her husband, and now like a sandcastle at the evening tide, it seemed as though her life had been washed away. Part of me still aches as I recall Melanie's deep cries of anguish that day and the circumstances that broke her tender heart.

Melanie isn't my only weeping friend, and I imagine that you also have at least one "Melanie" in your life. Many broken hearts in our neighborhoods, churches, and homes suffer under the heavy emotional burdens of sorrow, pain, and even despair. And sometimes we're the ones who weep. As I told a close friend recently, "We all have something that hurts us deeply."

God in Our Sorrow

This is the last of our chapters in which we provide specific Bible passages that you can share with those who are in need. It's been our delight to pore over the Scriptures and to consider truths to pass on to you so that you, in turn, can pass them on to others. Preparing and writing this chapter, however, has been of special concern to us. Perhaps it's because we've both known pain and loss, and we understand the anguish of personal sorrow. Perhaps it's because we've seen the ravages of grief in the lives of loved ones, and our hearts have broken with theirs. Maybe it's because we've wanted to be sensitive to the spiritual needs of you, our readers, who may have fresh wounds of your own. Or maybe it's because we know that even the best of our words ultimately can't provide the comfort and healing that those who are weeping desperately need.

Before looking at the following Scripture passages with us, there's an important point for you to consider when speaking truth in times of sorrow: your role in the lives of those who weep isn't to be their sole comforter; your role is to direct them to the Comforter of their souls. Yes, your kindness, your listening ear, your prayers, and your encouraging words will strengthen the sorrowful, but *your* comfort will never be enough. They need the comfort of God himself.

Susannah Spurgeon, wife of Charles Haddon Spurgeon, took this to heart. After the death of her husband, she could sympathize with those who mourned and suffered loss, but her greater purpose was to point them to the Lord and the consolation *he* provides. She wrote to a friend:

I quite understand your feelings, I have fellowship with you in your fear and faintness of heart; but I bring afresh to you, today, the sweet and comforting assurance that your blessed Lord knows all your sorrows, sees all your sufferings, is watching over you with a Divine love and care which knows no cessation, and will, in His own good time, either relieve or release you.[1]

Similarly, Joseph Scriven, an Irish immigrant whose life was characterized by repeated disappointment, wrote the precious hymn "What a Friend We Have in Jesus" to encourage his mother to turn to God for solace during her own time of sorrow:

What a friend we have in Jesus, all our sins and griefs to bear!
What a privilege to carry everything to God in prayer!
O what peace we often forfeit, O what needless pain we bear,
All because we do not carry everything to God in prayer![2]

Recently, I (Cheryl) woke up in the middle of the night, burdened with sadness. I tossed and turned, thought and prayed, and finally asked myself, "Who is God in my sorrow?" As I reminded myself of the ways that God—Father, Son, and Holy Spirit—cares for me in my sorrow, my soul was quieted, and I fell back asleep. As you prepare to speak truth to the weeping, to comfort them with the comfort of God, it's worthwhile for you to take a few minutes to ponder these questions: Who is God in our sorrow? Who is he when we weep at the death of a loved one? Who is he when we weep for a prodigal child? Who is he when we weep because of rejection or betrayal? Who is he when we weep over unrealized dreams and unfulfilled expectations? Who is God to his people when they grieve and mourn?

Jesus, God the Son, is the "man of sorrows and acquainted with grief," the one who has "carried our sorrows" (Isa. 53:3–4). He's our suffering Savior, who bore our sins and griefs on the cross. He's our compassionate high priest, who understands and sympathizes with our weaknesses, and through whom we have access to the throne of grace for help in our time of need (Heb. 4:16). Even now, he's our living Lord, who's preparing a place for us in heaven so that where he is, there we may also be (John 14:1–3).

As well, God the Spirit is our helper in times of sorrow. He's the Spirit of truth, given by the Father and Son to live within us and to be with us forever (John 14:16–17). He strengthens our faith as he teaches us the things of God, and fills us with wisdom, understanding, and hope (John 16:13; Eph. 1:17–19). When we're at a loss to know how to pray, the Spirit intercedes for us, and he assures us that we are beloved children of God (Rom. 8:16, 26).

And in our sorrow, God the Father is good *and* sovereign, equally perfect in both attributes. He's our good shepherd: he leads, restores, guides, comforts, and provides for us. His goodness and mercy will follow us all the days of our lives, even when we pass through the valley of death (Ps. 23). He's also our sovereign King, who rules over us and protects us in every circumstance: "For I, the LORD your God, hold your right hand;

it is I who say to you, 'Fear not, I am the one who helps you'"
(Isa. 41:13). We can rest our sorrowing hearts upon all these
truths now, but there's also a future and complete consolation
yet to be realized. All present comfort is but a small glimpse of
the everlasting joy that our Father God has reserved for us in
glory. At that time, he'll banish all sorrow, and we'll rejoice in
his presence forevermore:

> I heard a loud voice from the throne saying, "Behold, the dwell-
> ing place of God is with man. He will dwell with them, and
> they will be his people, and God himself will be with them as
> their God. He will wipe away every tear from their eyes, and
> death shall be no more, neither shall there be mourning, nor
> crying, nor pain anymore, for the former things have passed
> away." (Rev. 21:3–4)

The rest of this chapter contains three Bible passages with key
points and basic explanations, written as if addressed *directly to the
one who is in sorrow*. Choose one or more of these Scripture passages to share with or read to your sorrowing friend or loved one
and discuss the main points and explanations with her as you have
the opportunity. When you have conversations with the one who
weeps, remember that God is her all-sufficient Comforter and that
you're an instrument of his peace in her time of need. Consider
how you can lovingly serve her in her sorrow and compassionately
speak God's words of comfort and grace.

How Long, O Lord?

How long, O Lord? Will you forget me forever?
How long will you hide your face from me?

How long must I take counsel in my soul
  and have sorrow in my heart all the day?
How long shall my enemy be exalted over me?

Consider and answer me, O Lord my God;
  light up my eyes, lest I sleep the sleep of death,
lest my enemy say, "I have prevailed over him,"
  lest my foes rejoice because I am shaken.

But I have trusted in your steadfast love;
  my heart shall rejoice in your salvation.
I will sing to the Lord,
  because he has dealt bountifully with me. (Ps. 13:1–6)

1. Pour out your sorrow to the Lord.
  How long, O Lord? Will you forget me forever?
    How long will you hide your face from me?
  How long must I take counsel in my soul
    and have sorrow in my heart all the day?
  How long shall my enemy be exalted over me? (vv. 1–2)

When overcome by heartache, you may feel abandoned and alone. Perhaps God seems far away, and yet in reality he's near. You've not been forgotten by the Lord. He's within you, even closer than the trouble that breaks your heart. He knows your every thought, understands your every emotion, and accounts for every fallen tear. Like the psalmist, pour out your burdened heart to the Lord: "O God, I feel like you've forgotten and forsaken me. My soul aches, and I'm overwhelmed with grief. I can't bear the hurt I feel any longer. How long, O Lord, will I suffer in my sorrow?" Lay your soul before him, knowing that the Lord is near to the broken-hearted. He hasn't left or forsaken you.

2. Cry out to the Lord for help.

Consider and answer me, O LORD my God;
> light up my eyes, lest I sleep the sleep of death,
lest my enemy say, "I have prevailed over him,"
> lest my foes rejoice because I am shaken. (vv. 3–4)

As you pour out your heart to the Lord, cry out for his help in your sorrow. In desperate times of pain and loss we learn that only he can truly understand us and provide the spiritual and emotional aid we need. Perhaps like the psalmist you've cried out to the Lord, "Help me or I'll die!" Persevere in asking the Lord to "light up" your eyes—to give you the faith to see him and his faithfulness in the darkness of your sorrow. Pray for a steadfast hope in God that defies the enemy who wishes your faith to be destroyed. Resist the temptation to allow your heart to become hardened against the Lord. Cry out to him to strengthen your failing heart.

3. Trust the Lord in your sorrow as you have trusted him in your salvation.

But I have trusted in your steadfast love;
> my heart shall rejoice in your salvation. (v. 5)

The Lord never changes. He remains the same through all of life's circumstances. He's the Lord of steadfast love and the God of your salvation. He loves you with an everlasting love that can never be thwarted or diminished. The greatest expression of his love for you is the salvation he provided by the sacrifice of his Son. In love, he did not spare Christ but delivered him up for you. Does he not love you even now? He does—he *absolutely* does—and nothing can separate you from his love. As you trusted the Lord's love for your salvation, trust his love for you now in your sorrow. He still holds you in his strong and caring arms. Cling to the promises of his enduring love, and he will sustain you.

4. The Lord will restore your joy.

> I will sing to the LORD,
>> because he has dealt bountifully with me. (v. 6)

Loss, grief, and heartache have become your reality. But there's also another reality that exists, even though now it may be hard to see: the Lord has dealt bountifully with you in your suffering. He hasn't abandoned you; he's remained by your side and has cared for you in countless ways. Can you see him through your tears? Can you recognize the ways he's loved you in your sorrow? He's given you his salvation, his Spirit, and his word. He's given you daily reminders of his presence and provision. He's given you the hope of eternal life that exceeds your current circumstances. Can you thank him for these? Even if all you can do is whisper a simple word of praise in your weeping, then start there. Day by day as you begin to see the goodness of the Lord more clearly, he'll restore your joy and cause you to sing his praises once again. Make it your practice to thank the Lord for his bountiful gifts each new day.

Great Is Your Faithfulness

> Remember my affliction and my wanderings,
>> the wormwood and the gall!

My soul continually remembers it
   and is bowed down within me.
But this I call to mind,
   and therefore I have hope:

The steadfast love of the LORD never ceases;
   his mercies never come to an end;
they are new every morning;
   great is your faithfulness.
"The LORD is my portion," says my soul,
   "therefore I will hope in him."

The LORD is good to those who wait for him,
   to the soul who seeks him.
It is good that one should wait quietly
   for the salvation of the LORD. (Lam. 3:19–26)

I called on your name, O LORD. . . .
You came near when I called on you;
   you said, "Do not fear!"

You have taken up my cause, O Lord;
   you have redeemed my life. (Lam. 3:55–58)

*1. Even as a child of God, your grief may seem
overwhelming and impossible to bear.*
   Remember my affliction and my wanderings,
      the wormwood and the gall!
   My soul continually remembers it
      and is bowed down within me. (vv. 19–20)

In the book of Lamentations, the author wept over Jerusalem's fall to King Nebuchadnezzar and the Babylonians. The walls of the great city of David were destroyed, the temple was burned to the ground, and the people were decimated. His heart ached as he mourned the devastation that lay before him. Likewise, do you feel the misery, anguish, and bitterness of your loss? Do you feel as if your sorrow will never end? Are you overwhelmed by a grief that seems unbearable? Tell it all to the Lord. Lay your heart open before him. Know that the God of mercy and compassion hears and understands you.

2. The Lord's love for you is a faithful love.

> But this I call to mind,
>   and therefore I have hope:
>
> The steadfast love of the LORD never ceases;
>   his mercies never come to an end;
> they are new every morning;
>   great is your faithfulness. (vv. 21–23)

When experiencing intense sorrow, it's easy to fall into despair. It can be difficult to see the Lord's hand on your life and to hope in him. This is the time to redirect your thoughts to the Lord, to remember his eternal character and promises. Remind yourself—and if you're too weak, ask a friend to help you remember—that the Lord has always been and always will be your faithful and loving God. When others mistreat or abandon you, remember his steadfast love never ceases. When painful circumstances enter your life, remember his mercies are new every morning. When grief ravages your soul, remember his faithfulness is greater. Do you lack hope in your pain? Turn your mind to the Lord. Make a list of the countless ways God reveals his lovingkindness to you and then praise him for those blessings. Set your hope on God and remember his faithful love.

3. Your faithful God is your greatest good.

"The LORD is my portion," says my soul,
"therefore I will hope in him."

The LORD is good to those who wait for him,
to the soul who seeks him.
It is good that one should wait quietly
for the salvation of the LORD. (vv. 24–26)

When life doesn't go as planned, when dreams are unfulfilled, and when people disappoint, you will find that the Lord is your greatest good. He's your "portion" in life, more precious than the most treasured possession or inheritance. To say that God is good means that "all that God is and does is worthy of approval."[3] Nothing and no one can compare to the surpassing value of knowing him. His very presence is your good, and every gift from his hand is good. If it's hard for you to believe in the goodness of God right now, wait for him to reveal himself and to renew your faith. Seek him—patiently persist—in prayer and in his word, and he'll show your grieving heart his faithful character once again. The Lord will never cease loving you out of the deep well of his goodness.

4. Your Redeemer is always faithful.

I called on your name, O LORD. . . .
You came near when I called on you;
you said, "Do not fear!"

You have taken up my cause, O Lord;
  you have redeemed my life. (vv. 55–58)

The Lord hears you when you call upon him. He draws near to comfort and encourage you in your time of trouble. He understands the fears and questions that may accompany your sorrow: "What am I going to do? What will happen tomorrow or next week or next year? How will I make it through this?" Although you don't have the answers to all your questions, you can know this for certain: the Lord will be faithful to you every step of the way—you have no reason to fear. He's the Redeemer of your soul who has rescued you from sin and death and given you eternal life, and he won't fail you now. As you face your fears and doubts about the uncertainties of your future, take comfort in knowing that you're forever safe and secure in the Lord's presence. Take courage in knowing that the promises of his word will always be true. Do not fear, for great is his faithfulness.

The God of All Comfort

Blessed be the God and Father of our Lord Jesus Christ, the Father of mercies and God of all comfort, who comforts us in all our affliction, so that we may be able to comfort those who are in any affliction, with the comfort with which we ourselves are comforted by God. For as we share abundantly in Christ's sufferings, so through Christ we share abundantly in comfort too. . . . For we do not want you to be unaware, brothers, of the affliction we experienced in Asia. For we were so utterly burdened beyond our strength that we despaired of life itself. Indeed, we felt that we had received the sentence of death. But that was to make us rely not on ourselves but on God who raises the dead. He delivered us from such a deadly peril, and he will deliver us.

On him we have set our hope that he will deliver us again. You also must help us by prayer, so that many will give thanks on our behalf for the blessing granted us through the prayers of many. (2 Cor. 1:3–5, 8–11)

1. God is the God of all comfort who comforts you in every affliction.

Blessed be the God and Father of our Lord Jesus Christ, the Father of mercies and God of all comfort, who comforts us in all our affliction. (vv. 3–4)

God is the Father of mercies. He cares for you with a tender kindness, and his love for you is full of compassion. God is also the God of all comfort. Like no other, he comes alongside you to strengthen you when the burden of grief seems too much to bear. He's the "ultimate source of every true act of comfort."[4] He's the hand behind the friend who helps you, the truth behind the song that calms you, the Creator behind the nature that refreshes you, and the giver behind every gift that blesses you. His Spirit applies his word to your heart like a soothing balm, and he pours his peace into your soul like a cool river in a parched land. No affliction enters your life that doesn't have a corresponding comfort from the Lord. Receive his every consolation with a thankful heart.

2. God comforts you so that you can share his comfort with others.

. . . so that we may be able to comfort those who are in any affliction, with the comfort with which we ourselves are comforted by God. For as we share abundantly in Christ's sufferings, so through Christ we share abundantly in comfort too. (vv. 4–5)

As a child of God, your pain is never wasted. God always has good and wise purposes for your suffering. One of the reasons God permits sorrow in your life is so that you can share with others the comfort that he gives you. The compassion you receive from the Lord isn't only for your benefit but for the benefit of those who also sorrow. What is God teaching you in your suffering? Which of his promises have comforted your soul? Which scriptures have strengthened your heart? How do you understand and know God better than before? Share these comforts that God has given you with others who are also hurting. Be a messenger of his truth and grace according to their need—a need you now understand well. As followers of Christ, not only do we suffer together, but we also share in the abundant comfort he provides.

3. Suffering teaches you to rely on the God of comfort and not on yourself.

> We do not want you to be unaware, brothers, of the affliction we experienced in Asia. For we were so utterly burdened beyond our strength that we despaired of life itself. Indeed, we felt that we had received the sentence of death. But that was to make us rely not on ourselves but on God who raises the dead. He delivered us from such a deadly peril, and he will deliver us. On him we have set our hope that he will deliver us again. (vv. 8–10)

In these verses, Paul describes for the Corinthian church a severe trial he endured, and it was no small affliction. It pushed him beyond the limits of his own strength. He even thought he would die. Have you felt like that in your suffering? God's word will never minimize your trials, but it will provide their purpose. Here, Paul explains that his suffering was meant to teach him not to rely on himself but on God, who raises the dead. Your suffering and sorrow are meant to teach you the same thing: to rely on your all-powerful God and not yourself. Since God can raise the dead, he's more than able to help you in every difficult circumstance you encounter. What do you need to trust him for today? Commit it to him in prayer and entrust yourself to him by doing what is right. Set your hope on God, and you won't be disappointed.

4. God comforts you through the prayers of others.

You also must help us by prayer, so that many will give thanks on our behalf for the blessing granted us through the prayers of many. (v. 11)

Paul was committed to relying on the Lord instead of himself, and he was certain that God would deliver him from his troubles. He also understood that prayer gives voice to dependence on God, so he urged the Corinthians to join him in praying for his deliverance. Never be ashamed or timid to ask others to pray for you in your sorrow and suffering. It's a privilege and responsibility for believers to lift one another's concerns and needs to the Lord in prayer. It's also a tremendous blessing to share in giving thanks to God for prayers that have been answered. Prayer is a gift from the God of all comfort. He consoles us in private prayer, but he greatly multiplies our joy when we pray together and then see him move. It's in prayer for one another that we can truly rejoice with those who rejoice and weep with those who weep.

REFLECTION QUESTIONS

1. Spend time rereading and thoroughly familiarizing yourself with the scriptures and key points presented in this chapter.

2. Which of these Bible passages is the most meaningful to you and why? What does it teach you about God? What does it teach you about yourself? How might it impact what you believe or how you live?

3. Is there another Bible passage or verse that the Lord has used in your own life to comfort you? What truth have you personally learned from it that you could share with a weeping friend?

4. Read Psalm 40. Underline five verses in this psalm that you think would be an encouragement to someone in sorrow. Make your own notes about what those verses say about the Lord and how he cares for his people.

5. Proverbs 15:23 says, "To make an apt answer is a joy to a man, and a word in season, how good it is!" Do you have a friend who's enduring a season of weeping and needs a word of comfort? How can you love her in a practical way (such as sharing a meal, listening as she processes her grief, writing out encouraging Bible verses for her, walking together in a beautiful place)? Pray for your friend, and whether it be in a conversation or a written note, share with her a relevant Scripture passage from this chapter. Comfort her with God's truth in love.

11

Our Confidence to Speak

Such is the confidence that we have through Christ toward
God. Not that we are sufficient in ourselves to claim
anything as coming from us, but our sufficiency is from God.

2 CORINTHIANS 3:4–5

AS WE BEGIN THIS LAST CHAPTER, our hearts are full of gratitude. We thank the Lord that we've been able to share with you
some of the lessons we've learned about building up others with his
word and some of the experiences we've had putting those lessons
into practice. We're also grateful that you've joined our journey
through this book and have persevered to its end. Our aim has
been to encourage and equip you to speak truth with grace into
the lives of those you love according to their need, and we trust
that you're now better prepared to share his word with whomever
he places in your path.

We began the book by looking at God's call for each of us to
speak his truth to others so that they as individuals, and the church

as a whole, may be built up in love to the glory of Christ. We then considered the people that God has placed within our unique spheres of influence and how we ought to respond to them by admonishing the unruly, encouraging the fainthearted, and helping the weak. Knowing that God doesn't simply call us to speak truth but to speak truth *in love*, we then explored the grace of God toward each of us through Christ and how our personal knowledge and experience of his grace should motivate and shape how we share his truth with others—always with grace.

Next, we turned our attention to the actual truth that God calls us to speak. That truth is his word, and it is powerful to transform the lives of those who receive it by faith. The Scriptures teach, reprove, correct, and train us to live righteously for God, and they'll accomplish in our lives every good purpose that he intends. So we provided several passages of Scripture that you can personally share with friends and loved ones who are worried, weary, wayward, or weeping. God's word will grow them in Christlikeness. You can wholeheartedly trust his word to do its life-changing work in those who believe.

As you've read our stories about how we've come alongside others to build them up with God's word, we hope you've thought of people in your own life who also need to be lovingly admonished, encouraged, and helped from the Scriptures. It's no accident that God has put you in their lives and that he's placed this book into your hands. He's given you real-life opportunities and practical instruction to contribute to the building up of his church by speaking truth in love. Now is the time for you to speak. But perhaps you still don't feel ready to have a conversation in which you share Scripture and biblical truth with another person. We'll let you in on a secret—you'll never feel ready enough. You'll never feel wise enough. You'll never feel confident enough. And for that reason, we have one more story to share with you.

The Insufficient Shepherd

Forty years had passed since Moses had last seen the Nile River running through Egypt, his childhood home. Once welcomed in Pharaoh's royal court, Moses had become a fugitive in the faraway wilderness of Midian. After murdering an Egyptian who had beaten an Israelite slave, Moses had fled to escape the justice of Pharaoh. In the many years since, Moses had built a new life as a shepherd and begun a family of his own. Time had not removed the sting of being separated from his Israelite family and the enslaved tribes of his forefathers. He even named his first son Gershom, meaning "foreigner," saying, "I have been a sojourner in a foreign land" (Ex. 2:22).

One day when Moses was tending his father-in-law's flock on Mount Horeb, the Lord appeared to him in a burning bush and said:

> I am the God of your father, the God of Abraham, the God of Isaac, and the God of Jacob. . . . I have surely seen the affliction of my people who are in Egypt and have heard their cry because of their taskmasters. . . . And now, behold, the cry of the people of Israel has come to me, and I have also seen the oppression with which the Egyptians oppress them. Come, I will send you to Pharaoh that you may bring my people, the children of Israel, out of Egypt. (Ex. 3:6–7, 9–10)

Now, you would think that upon hearing the voice of the Lord, Moses would immediately reply like the prophet Isaiah, who spoke centuries later when he encountered God: "Here I am! Send me" (Isa. 6:8). But no, not Moses. When God called him to return to Egypt and speak on his behalf to the Israelites and Pharaoh, he repeatedly questioned the Lord. And the Lord in turn patiently answered each of Moses's objections.

Our own reasons to avoid speaking God's truth to others often sound a lot like Moses's reasons to avoid speaking to Pharaoh and the Israelites. Today God teaches us the same lessons about himself that he taught Moses long ago. Our confidence to speak truth with grace to one another is rooted in knowing that God is present, powerful, and faithful to his promises. Let's look together at Moses's reasons for his reluctance and God's answers to each of them. Then we'll consider what they mean for us today.

The Lord Is with You

When God told Moses that his plan was to send him back to Egypt to bring the Israelites out of slavery, Moses made his first objection: "Who am I that I should go to Pharaoh and bring the children of Israel out of Egypt?" (Ex. 3:11). Surely God had made a mistake! Why should Moses be the one to go? How could he, a fugitive shepherd, be the right choice for such a monumental task? God didn't answer Moses's question directly. He didn't reassure Moses of any personal qualities or experience that qualified him for the assignment. Instead, he focused Moses's attention on the foundational truth he needed to know first and foremost: "I will be with you" (Ex. 3:12).

As you consider speaking biblical truth into the life of someone with a spiritual need, you might wonder like Moses, "Who am I that I should go and talk with her about that? I feel so inadequate to say anything." Remember the promise Jesus gave before his ascension: "Go therefore and make disciples of all nations . . . teaching them to observe all that I have commanded you. And behold, I am with you always, to the end of the age" (Matt. 28:19–20). In the context of commanding us to speak his truth to others, Jesus promises his presence. He's with us to help us—to give courage, wisdom, and grace—so that we may complete the task he's placed before us. Just as God promised to be with Moses, Christ promises to be with you as well. Have confidence that he's present as you share his word.

The Lord Has Sent You

Moses then raised a second objection: "If I come to the people of Israel and say to them, 'The God of your fathers has sent me to you,' and they ask me, 'What is his name?' what shall I say to them?" (Ex. 3:13). In other words, Moses was concerned that they'd ask him by whose authority he had come to them; what would he say? God replied, "Say this to the people of Israel: 'I AM has sent me to you. . . . The LORD, the God of your fathers, the God of Abraham, of Isaac, and of Jacob, has appeared to me, saying, "I have observed you and what has been done to you in Egypt, and I promise that I will bring you up out of the affliction of Egypt"'" (Ex. 3:14, 16–17). God was explaining that Moses would not be approaching the Israelites or Pharaoh based on any authority or message of his own. Rather, Moses would speak to them the word of God by the authority of God. Moses would communicate *God's* message.

Perhaps you realize that someone you care about needs the help provided in God's word, but you feel awkward or afraid to say anything. You may question, "What right do I have to speak into her life? I'm no authority on the issues she's facing." Understand that God has providentially placed you into her life and made you aware of her need. Also know that God's purpose isn't for you to give her your own wisdom, but to build her up with God's wisdom. Approach her with a humble confidence in Scripture as the source of the encouragement or exhortation you share and the authority by which you share it.

The Lord Will Validate His Word

At this point in the conversation, Moses stopped asking questions. He moved on to making assumptions. He continued, "But behold, they will not believe me or listen to my voice, for they will say, 'The LORD did not appear to you'" (Ex. 4:1). Moses assumed the worst. Nobody would listen to him. Nobody would receive what he had to say. He might as well not even try. It's hard to imagine how surprised Moses must have been at God's response:

> The LORD said to him, "What is that in your hand?" He said, "A staff." And he said, "Throw it on the ground." So he threw it on the ground, and it became a serpent, and Moses ran from it. But the LORD said to Moses, "Put out your hand and catch it by the tail"—so he put out his hand and caught it, and it became a staff in his hand—"that they may believe that the LORD, the God of their fathers, the God of Abraham, the God of Isaac, and the God of Jacob, has appeared to you." (Ex. 4:2–5)

What did God prove to Moses? He is all-powerful. There's absolutely nothing too difficult for God. If he could turn a staff into a snake—give life to an inanimate object—couldn't he turn the hearts of his people to hear and believe Moses? This miracle displayed God's sovereign power, showing Moses that God was able to authenticate both his messenger and his message. Moses simply had to trust and obey and then leave the results to God. No matter what opposition or resistance Moses would face, God was mighty to fulfill his purposes and validate his word.

Like Moses, you might be tempted to assume that the truth you speak won't be received well: "I know she won't listen to me, and she probably won't like what I say. I'll make a fool of myself!" Your concerns about how she responds to you or your biblical counsel shouldn't keep you from speaking truth. Your primary concern should be to obey God by graciously speaking truth according to her need. The Lord is powerful to validate in her heart and life the scriptures you share. You might not see an immediate, positive response from her, but that's alright. God is working all things together for her good, including your conversations with her. He will apply his word to her life in his own way and time.

The Lord Will Teach You

You might think that Moses would now finally surrender to the Lord, but he was still unsure that he could do what God had called him to do. The great I am had been speaking to Moses through a burning bush and had easily dismantled every objection he had raised, and yet Moses continued to object: "Oh, my Lord, I am not eloquent, either in the past or since you have spoken to your servant, but I am slow of speech and of tongue" (Ex. 4:10).

Like us, you might wonder what Moses meant by that. Did he have a speech impediment? Was he afraid of public speaking? Did he find the language of Egypt too difficult after so many years in exile? Whatever the case, God didn't view Moses's lack of eloquence as an obstacle. God directed Moses to put his confidence in his all-wise Creator. The Lord said, "Who has made man's mouth? Who makes him mute, or deaf, or seeing, or blind? Is it not I, the LORD? Now therefore go, and I will be with your mouth and teach you what you shall speak" (Ex. 4:11–12).

Have you ever felt like Moses? "Lord, I'm not very good at talking, especially about someone's problems. I'm not even sure what to say. I'm really not cut out for this." Your concern is very common and understandable. However, the one who made you and knows your weaknesses still commands you to speak his truth in love, and he'll always give you the help you need to obey him. God created you and has sovereignly given you your own unique ability to communicate with others. Even more importantly, he's given you his Spirit to teach you the truth of his word. And just as the Lord taught the psalmist, he'll also teach you his wisdom so that you can pass it on to those who need to hear it: "Behold, you delight in truth in the inward being, and you teach me wisdom in the secret heart. . . . I will teach transgressors your ways, and sinners will return to you" (Ps. 51:6, 13).

The Lord Will Provide

Moses made one last attempt to convince God that he wasn't the one to speak for him. It wasn't really an objection as much as it was a blatant refusal to obey: "Oh, my Lord, please send someone else" (Ex. 4:13). There was nothing left for Moses to say but "No, God, I'm not going to do this. Go find someone else who will." God didn't respond lightly: "Then the anger of the LORD was kindled against Moses" (Ex. 4:14).

God had patiently given Moses every explanation and assurance necessary for Moses to speak on his behalf to Pharaoh and the Israelites, yet Moses still resisted the Lord's command. Although the Lord was angry with Moses's stubborn unbelief, he graciously provided Moses with what *Moses* thought he needed—someone else to do the talking. God answered, "Is there not Aaron, your brother, the Levite? I know that he can speak well. . . . You shall speak to him and put the words in his mouth, and I will be with your mouth and with his mouth and will teach you both what to do" (Ex. 4:14–15). Even though God provided Aaron to assist Moses, Moses wasn't off the hook and God's plan wasn't thwarted. Moses would still speak on God's behalf. Moses would give the word of the Lord to Aaron, and Aaron would help him convey that message to the people. God provided a way for Moses to obey.

Is there someone you care about who needs to hear God's truth, but maybe you're rationalizing that you personally don't have to be the one to speak with her? Perhaps you've even gone to the next step in your mind of flatly refusing. Maybe you've said to yourself, "I don't want to talk with her about her situation. I have good reasons to not say anything or get involved. I'm sure someone else will do it, but it won't be me." Your rationalizations and excuses will never remove your God-given responsibility to build up others in the body of Christ. His intention is for you to communicate truth in love for the good of his people. Speaking with others is the primary way for you to do this, but there are other means available to help you in this task: offering to read through Scripture together, giving your friend a helpful booklet, suggesting she listen to a sermon or podcast, or connecting her to another strong believer who has walked her road.

Trust the Lord to help you overcome the doubts and weaknesses that hinder you from sharing his word with those in need. The Lord will faithfully provide the opportunities, instruction, and encouragement you need to confidently speak truth with grace into the lives of those you love.

Our Sufficiency Is from God

In response to each of the five objections raised by Moses, God showed him that he would provide everything Moses lacked. God would provide Moses with his presence, power, and whatever was needed to fulfill what he had called Moses to do. You know the rest of the story. Moses returned to Egypt and eventually led the Israelites out of their captivity and to the promised land. Through all the challenges of leading God's people, Moses learned to put his confidence in the Lord. Time and again God proved himself trustworthy by leading Moses in the way he should go and providing Moses with the words to speak. God was always faithful, just as he had promised.

The Lord promises you the same—his presence, power, and provision—so that you may faithfully speak truth in love for the building up of his people. *He* will be with you. *He* will send you to those in need. *He* will validate the truth you share. *He* will teach you what to say. *He* will provide whatever you need in order to obey. *He* alone is your confidence to speak.

Paul explained his confidence when he wrote, "Such is the confidence that we have through Christ toward God. Not that we are sufficient in ourselves to claim anything as coming from us, but our sufficiency is from God" (2 Cor. 3:4–5). His confidence was in God's ability, and not his own. As you recognize your inadequacies to speak God's truth, remember that the almighty God, the great I am, the Lord of heaven and earth, is with you and infinitely powerful to enable you to speak his truth with grace. Your sufficiency is found only in the Lord whom you serve. He's placed the treasure of his word in you, a common and fragile jar of clay, so that as his word is poured out, he's the one who is praised (2 Cor. 4:7).

There's Only One Savior
We want to leave you with one final thought to encourage you as you speak truth with grace. It's rather obvious and yet profoundly

relevant: there's only one Savior—and you're not him. Jesus is the one who saves and sanctifies his people, and that was never a weight intended for you to carry. You can't rescue anyone, but Christ can. You can't change anyone, but Christ can. You don't have the power to produce spiritual life and transformation in those you love, but you can have every confidence that Christ does.

Jesus said, "*I* will build *my* church" (Matt. 16:18). He loves his church, his redeemed people, his bride, with an everlasting love. The Lord laid aside his glory for her, died in her place, and lives again for her. He cleanses her, intercedes for her, and will never forsake her. Until Jesus gathers her to himself, he's preparing a home for her and preparing her for her future home. In the meantime, he's promised to build his church, and he won't leave that work undone. Jesus will complete what he started—the salvation, sanctification, and glorification of his people.

The Lord has built his church on the foundation of the apostles and prophets, and that bedrock is the word of God proclaimed long ago. Jesus continues to build his church on his word today, transforming lives with his eternal truth. In his grand design, you're also a builder. He's entrusted you with the high calling of speaking his word to others for the building up of his church. Our prayer is that the meditations of your heart—and the words of your mouth—will be pleasing to him, your rock and Redeemer.

REFLECTION QUESTIONS

---

1. Read Exodus 2:23–4:20. Describe a time when you felt as Moses did in these verses. Explain your circumstances. What did you think and why? What did you do or not do as a result? Which of

God's answers to Moses give you confidence to apply what you have learned in this book?

2. Read 2 Corinthians 3:4–8 and 4:1–7. What do you see as your inadequacies as you consider sharing God's word with those in need? Which of those inadequacies are too difficult for God to overcome? According to these verses, why was Paul so confident in his ministry to others?

3. Which chapter in this book did you find the most helpful to you? Explain why. What changes will you make in your conversations as a result of reading that chapter?

4. Explain what is meant by this statement on page 52: "Speaking truth with grace begins with receiving and knowing the grace of God in our own lives." How would this statement apply to your own life? Are there aspects of your speech you believe need to change because of your knowledge and experience of God's grace?

5. The final paragraph states: "In [Jesus's] grand design, you're also a builder." Explain this analogy in your own words. What scriptures can be used to prove this point? Make a list of a few women you know who need spiritual encouragement and create a plan for how you will build them up with truth and grace.

Acknowledgments

Cheryl

It's hard for me to believe that I'm writing acknowledgments for a book. This endeavor has been outside my comfort zone, far beyond anything I could ask or think. But here I am, and I couldn't be more grateful.

Thank you, Caroline Newheiser, for writing *When Words Matter Most* with me. When the book's premise was just a spark, I knew I wanted you to be a part of it. As I expected, your biblical wisdom, counseling experience, and compassionate heart fanned the spark into a flame. I'll always look back on this experience with you with a special fondness, and I'll miss our many phone discussions, late-night texts, and times of praying together for the Lord to grant us wisdom and to use this book for the building of his church. Thank you, dear friend.

Thank you, Dave DeWit, for believing that Caroline and I had something to say and that we could say it. Your encouraging words and helpful critique throughout the writing process gave us confidence and courage to stay the course. I'm grateful for your kindness each step of the way, and I pray this book will be as helpful to others as you have hoped it would be. Thank you, Lydia Brownback, for your editorial advice in the final stages of the manuscript. I'm grateful to have learned from your expertise.

Thank you, Dana Wilkerson, for editing our original proposal chapters. Our first conversation on the phone was a lifesaver for this book. You were the answer to my specific prayers for a freelance editor—a woman highly experienced in writing and theologically trained. The Lord knew we needed you, and he provided you at just the right time.

Thank you, Jim Newheiser, for introducing me to biblical counseling twenty-five years ago. What you taught back then I've carried with me all these years, and it's impacted my marriage, parenting, friendships, and ministry. This book would never have been written without the care and training you provided your seminary interns and their wives many years ago. Thank you for reading the manuscript and providing many beneficial comments. And, of course, thank you for letting me steal Caroline's attention for a while!

Thank you, my sweet praying friends and family, the small army of women scattered across the United States from Delaware to California, who have prayed many months for the writing of this book. The fruit of your prayers is found on its pages, and I trust that many will feast because of your unseen labor.

Thank you, Richard Caldwell, because your influence is also found on these pages. Your faithful preaching of God's word from week to week has provided me with an invaluable example of how to think carefully about Scripture and how to effectively communicate and apply it to the heart.

Thank you, Frank and Leona Lott, for being loving, encouraging, and sacrificial parents. Thank you for introducing me to Jesus forty-five years ago. Thank you for taking me to a church that preached the word and for providing me with a Christian education. I'm grateful for the countless ways you have encouraged and supported me. What you have poured in, I have sought to pour out.

Thank you, John-Phillip, Kathryn, and Andrew, for the joy you bring to me as your mom. Thank you for your patience with me after late nights of writing, your help around the house, your humor that keeps me laughing, and your willingness to discuss God's word. I pray that you'll always treasure the truth you have received and learn to graciously share it with others in their time of need.

And, Phillip, thank you. There's so much to say that I really don't know where to start or where to end. What I do know is this: I couldn't have done this without you. You've been my sounding board, cheerleader, computer technician, grammar teacher, proofreader, personal assistant, prayer partner, counselor, pastor, friend, and better half. Thank you for making this book possible. I love you.

Finally, I thank the Lord for the amazing opportunity to coauthor this book, for the many people who have helped make it a reality, and for the life-changing truth and grace of which Caroline and I have written. Our words will fall short, but his never will.

Caroline

When Words Matter Most is a labor of love, built on the foundational truths of the gospel.

I would characterize its contents as "the gospel applied to life." In my own walk with the Lord, I have experienced Moses's declaration that Scripture "is no empty word for you, but your very life" (Deut. 32:47), and so this book about the life-giving word comes from my heart. I'm thankful for the opportunity to humbly share how I have personally experienced the power of God's word and have seen its effect in the lives of the women you have read about here.

This project would not have been possible without the support and encouragement of many who have been used by the Lord in my life. It began when Cheryl Marshall contacted me with the idea to write a book to help women speak biblical truth to others who are struggling spiritually. The Bible has been an effective source of strength in my own journey, and I have wanted to share that blessing with others. But it was Cheryl who had the vision, drive, and talent to bring this book to fruition. Our friendship has only grown stronger as we have worked alongside each other. For that I give thanks to the Lord, and I also thank Cheryl for graciously including me in this project.

Many thanks belong to Dave DeWit and Crossway for taking a chance on us. Dave made himself available to give helpful advice and answer questions as they came up. His encouragement kept us going. Thank you to Lydia Brownback for her helpful edits and suggestions. Also, I appreciate the desire of the editors at Crossway to provide biblical materials for female readers.

Early on, Martha Peace read a few chapters and offered feedback and encouragement. I'm grateful that she saw the potential for this book to be useful to women in the church. Martha also deserves thanks for her example of selfless service to and mentoring of many women, including me.

My husband, Jim, sacrificed enjoying our time together and several of my home-cooked meals as each writing deadline approached. He regularly gave a listening ear and theological insights when Cheryl and I needed clarity. He continues to be my cheerleader. All through our marriage, Jim has encouraged me to serve the Lord in ways beyond what I could have imagined for myself. Thank you, Jim!

Finally, the Lord has brought many precious women into my life who have contributed in their own ways to this book. My heart has broken as I have watched some of them struggle through difficult real-life situations. Others have strengthened my spiritual walk by setting an example and exhorting me to change. With each friend, I have learned more about how to use my words to point them to a deeper relationship with our Lord and Savior. Soli Deo Gloria.

Recommended Resources

For the Worried

Caldwell, Richard. *Answering Anxiety: A Biblical Answer for What Troubles Your Heart.* The Woodlands, TX: Kress, 2017.

Fitzpatrick, Elyse. *Overcoming Fear, Worry, and Anxiety: Becoming a Woman of Faith and Confidence.* Eugene, OR: Harvest, 2001.

MacArthur, John. *Anxious for Nothing: God's Cure for the Cares of Your Soul.* Colorado Springs, CO: David C. Cook, 2012.

Mack, Wayne A., and Joshua Mack. *Courage: Fighting Fear with Fear.* Phillipsburg, NJ: P&R, 2014.

Welch, Edward T. *Running Scared: Fear, Worry, and the God of Rest.* Greensboro, NC: New Growth Press, 2007.

For the Weary

Carson, D. A. *How Long, O Lord?: Reflections on Suffering and Evil.* Grand Rapids, MI: Baker Academic, 2006.

Fitzpatrick, Elyse, and Dennis Johnson. *Counsel from the Cross: Connecting Broken People to the Love of Christ.* Wheaton, IL: Crossway, 2012.

Mack, Wayne A., and Deborah Howard. *It's Not Fair!—Finding Hope When Times Are Tough.* Phillipsburg, NJ: P&R, 2008.

Meyer, Jason. *Don't Lose Heart: Gospel Encouragement for the Weary Soul.* Grand Rapids, MI: Baker, 2019.

Powlison, David. *I'm Exhausted: What to Do When You're Always Tired*. Greensboro, NC: New Growth Press, 2010.

For the Wayward

Bridges, Jerry. *The Pursuit of Holiness*. Colorado Springs, CO: Nav-Press, 2016.

———. *Respectable Sins*. Colorado Springs, CO: NavPress, 2017.

Newheiser, Jim. *Help! I Want to Change*. Wapwallopen, PA: Shepherd Press, 2014.

———. "Seven Traits of True Repentance/Seven Traits of Worldly Sorrow." Counseling card. *Jim Newheiser* website. Accessed January 19, 2021. https://jimnewheiser.com/counseling-cards-english/.

Sande, Ken. *The Peacemaker*. Grand Rapids, MI: Baker, 2004.

Scott, Stuart, with Zondra Scott. *Killing Sin Habits: Conquering Sin with Radical Faith*. Bemidji, MN: Focus, 2013.

For the Weeping

Kellemen, Bob. *Grief: Walking with Jesus* (31-Day Devotionals for Life). Phillipsburg, NJ: P&R, 2018.

Lloyd-Jones, Martyn. *Spiritual Depression: Its Causes and Its Cure*. Grand Rapids, MI: Zondervan, 1998.

Newheiser, Jim. "Eight Truths against the Lies of Sadness." Counseling card. *Jim Newheiser* website. Accessed January 19, 2021. https://jimnewheiser.com/counseling-cards-english/.

Tada, Joni Eareckson, and Steve Estes. *When God Weeps*. Grand Rapids, MI: Zondervan, 1997.

Vroegop, Mark. *Dark Clouds, Deep Mercy: Discovering the Grace of Lament*. Wheaton, IL: Crossway, 2019.

Notes

Preface

1. Cecilia Kang, "The Humble Phone Call Has Made a Comeback," *New York Times*, April 9, 2020, https://www.nytimes.com/2020/04/09/technology/phone-calls-voice-virus.html.

Chapter 1: The Call to Speak

1. Bill Mounce, *Greek Dictionary*, s.v. "oikodome," accessed February 27, 2019, http://www.billmounce.com/greek-dictionary/oikodome/.

2. "How Firm a Foundation, Ye Saints of the Lord," *Hymnary*, accessed February 27, 2019, https://hymnary.org/text/how_firm_a_foundation _ye_saints_of.

Chapter 2: Those We Love

1. "500 Greatest Songs of all Time," *Rolling Stone*, accessed March 15, 2019, https://www.rollingstone.com/music/music-lists/500-greatest-songs-of -all-time-151127/bill-withers-lean-on-me-53629/.

2. Philip Ryken, *Galatians*, Reformed Expository Commentary (Phillipsburg, NJ: P&R, 2005), 248.

3. W. E. Vines, Merrill F. Unger, William White Jr., *Vine's Complete Expository Dictionary of Old and New Testament Words* (Nashville, TN: Thomas Nelson, 1996), s.v. "Disorderly."

4. Vines, Unger, and White, *Vine's Complete Expository Dictionary*, s.v. "Admonition, Admonish."

5. Vines, Unger, and White, *Vine's Complete Expository Dictionary*, s.v. "Fainthearted."

6. Vines, Unger, and White, *Vine's Complete Expository Dictionary*, s.v. "Comfort, Comforter, Comfortless."

7. John Charles Ryle, *Expository Thoughts on the Gospels*, vol. 3, *St. John* (New York: Robert Carter & Brothers, 1874), 406.

8. Vines, Unger, and White, *Vine's Complete Expository Dictionary*, s.v. "Weak, Weakened, Weaker, Weakness."

9. Vines, Unger, and White, *Vine's Complete Expository Dictionary*, s.v. "Hold (Down, Fast, Forth, On, To, Up), Held, Holden, (Take) Hold."

Chapter 3: The Greater Grace

1. Julia H. Johnston, "Grace Greater than All Our Sin," *Hymnary*, accessed April 15, 2019, https://hymnary.org/text/marvelous_grace_of _our_loving_lord.

2. Billy Graham, *Nearing Home: Life, Faith, and Finishing Well* (Nashville, TN: Thomas Nelson, 2011), 95.

3. Wayne Grudem, *Systematic Theology* (Grand Rapids, MI: Zondervan, 1994), 746.

4. For more about the process of sanctification, we recommend Jim Newheiser, *Help! I Want to Change* (Wapwallopen, PA: Shepherd Press, 2014).

5. For a thorough discussion about the different aspects of sanctification found in Scripture, we recommend John Murray, *Collected Writings of John Murray, vol. 2: Selected Lectures in Systematic Theology* (Edinburgh, UK: Banner of Truth, 1977), 277–317.

6. Grudem, *Systematic Theology*, 828.

Chapter 4: The Gracious Friend

1. John MacArthur, *The MacArthur Study Bible* (Nashville, TN: Thomas Nelson, 2006), note on Eph. 5:18.

2. For more about humility, we recommend Stuart Scott, *From Pride to Humility: A Biblical Perspective* (Bemidji, MN: Focus, 2002).

3. *Merriam-Webster*, s.v. "loyalty," accessed September 29, 2019, https:// www.merriam-webster.com/thesaurus/loyalty.

4. Matthew Henry, *Matthew Henry's Commentary on the Whole Bible: Complete and Unabridged in One Volume* (Peabody, MA: Hendrickson, 1994), 1016.

5. *Merriam-Webster*, s.v. "self-control," accessed September 29, 2019, https://www.merriam-webster.com/dictionary/self-control.

6. This question is the subject of a poem in Mary Ann Pietzker, *Miscellaneous Poems* (London: Griffith & Farran, 1872), 55.

7. For more about biblical conflict resolution, we recommend Ken Sande, *The Peacemaker* (Grand Rapids, MI: Baker, 2004).

8. *Merriam-Webster*, s.v. "wise," accessed September 29, 2019, https://www .merriam-webster.com/dictionary/wise.

9. Sinclair Ferguson, *Grow in Grace* (Edinburgh, UK: Banner of Truth, 1989), 29.

10. R. C. Sproul, *The Purpose of God: Ephesians* (Fearn, Ross-shire, UK: Christian Focus, 1994), 40.

11. Lucy Maud Montgomery, *Anne of Green Gables* (Hertfordshire, UK: Wordsworth Editions Limited, 1994), 59.

12. These points about forgiveness are explained in Ken Sande and Kevin Johnson, *Resolving Everyday Conflict* (Grand Rapids, MI: Baker, 2011), 52–93. For more about forgiveness, we recommend Stephen Viars, *Putting Your Past in Its Place: Moving Forward in Freedom and Forgiveness* (Eugene, OR: Harvest, 2011).

Chapter 5: When Grace Is Tested

1. For more about anger, we recommend Robert D. Jones, *Uprooting Anger: Biblical Help for a Common Problem* (Phillipsburg, NJ: P&R, 2005) and Jim Newheiser, *Help! My Anger Is Out of Control* (Wapwallopen, PA: Shepherd Press, 2015).

2. For more about church discipline, we recommend Jay E. Adams, *Handbook of Church Discipline: A Right and Privilege of Every Church Member* (Grand Rapids, MI: Zondervan, 1986).

Chapter 6: Truth That Transforms

1. For a resource about the nature of Scripture, we recommend Kevin DeYoung, *Taking God at His Word: Why the Bible Is Knowable, Necessary, and Enough, and What That Means for You and Me* (Wheaton, IL: Crossway, 2016).

2. Wayne Grudem, *Systematic Theology* (Grand Rapids, MI: Zondervan, 1994), 81.

3. Grudem, *Systematic Theology*, 91; emphasis original.

4. Matthew Henry, *Matthew Henry's Commentary on the Whole Bible: Complete and Unabridged* (Peabody, MA: Hendrickson, 2008), 1896; emphasis original.

5. For a resource on studying Scripture, we recommend Jen Wilkin, *Women of the Word: How to Study the Bible with Both Our Hearts and Our Minds* (Wheaton, IL: Crossway, 2019).

Chapter 7: Truth for the Worried

1. *Merriam-Webster*, s.v. "worry," accessed December 7, 2019, https://www.merriam-webster.com/dictionary/worry.

2. Helen Howarth Lemmel, "Turn Your Eyes upon Jesus," *Hymnary*, accessed November 29, 2019, https://hymnary.org/text/o_soul_are_you_weary_and_troubled.

Chapter 8: Truth for the Weary

1. John MacArthur, *The MacArthur Study Bible* (Nashville, TN: Thomas Nelson, 2006), note on Rom. 5:3.
2. Matthew Henry, *Matthew Henry's Commentary on the Whole Bible: Complete and Unabridged in One Volume* (Peabody, MA: Hendrickson, 1994), 1152.
3. Eric Metaxas, *Seven Women and the Secret of Their Greatness* (Nashville, TN: Thomas Nelson, 2015), 41.
4. MacArthur, *MacArthur Study Bible*, note on 2 Cor. 4:18.

Chapter 9: Truth for the Wayward

1. For more about how to restore the wayward, we recommend "Gently Restore," in Ken Sande, *The Peacemaker* (Grand Rapids, MI: Baker, 2004), 139–200.
2. *Strong's Hebrew Lexicon (ESV)*, s.v. "H3474 yashar," accessed February 14, 2020, https://www.blueletterbible.org/lang/lexicon/lexicon.cfm?t=ESV&strongs=h3474.
3. For a resource on the role of confession in repentance, we recommend "Confession Brings Freedom," in Sande, *Peacemaker*, 117–37.

Chapter 10: Truth for the Weeping

1. Ray Rhodes Jr., *Susie: The Life and Legacy of Susannah Spurgeon* (Chicago: Moody, 2018), 197.
2. Joseph Scriven, "What a Friend We Have in Jesus," *Hymnary*, accessed April 16, 2020, https://hymnary.org/text/what_a_friend_we_have_in_jesus_all_our_s.
3. Wayne Grudem, *Systematic Theology* (Grand Rapids, MI: Zondervan, 1994), 197.
4. John MacArthur, *The MacArthur Study Bible* (Nashville, TN: Thomas Nelson, 2006), note on 2 Cor. 1:3.

General Index

Scripture Index